CW00524080

First Published in the United States of America, 2014

First Edition

Gingko Press, Inc.
1321 Fifth Street
Berkeley, CA 94710, USA
www.gingkopress.com

ISBN: 978-1-58423-538-5

All photos taken by the author using an old brick sized Canon
Power Shot S410

Printed in China.

CONTENTS

INTRODUCTION

I've always been fascinated by records. As a kid, I can remember sitting in my father's room watching him play records for hours. He'd carefully remove each record from its sleeve, making sure that his fingers didn't touch the vinyl. He was very serious about not getting fingerprints on the records. He would always say, "Fingerprints ruin the record; don't get fingerprints on the record." Then, he'd carefully clean the record he'd just taken out of the sleeve with one of the multiple dust removing tools he always had lying next to his turntable. Once the record was clean, he'd take one of the cleaning tools and slide it under the needle to make sure he cleaned any dust out from under it. This meticulous ritual happened every single time he'd play a record. Sitting there as a kid, listening to the music play through the speakers, I was in heaven. Naturally I wanted to play some records, too. So I'd go through his LPs and pull something out of his stash that caught my eye, something that looked really interesting to me, and ask him to play it. I was about five or six years old at the time and my brother was just a little older than I was, and sometimes when Dad wasn't home we'd go through his collection, turn the stereo on and play records like we were slick. Of course he'd eventually find out, and sometimes we'd be punished for playing his records without permission. But those were good times, and now I can blame my father for my record addiction; ultimately my love of records developed from those hours spent sitting with him, listening to his records.

By the time I got to the eighth grade I started buying my own records and building a collection of my own. I think the first record I ever bought was Rodney O & Joe Cooley's "Me & Joe" for around two bucks at a local record shop. I probably wouldn't play that record much today, as my tastes have grown significantly over the years. But at the time, in 1989/1990, I played the hell out of that record. That same year I got my first pair of turntables and DJing parties (mostly for the girls) became my mission.

Skip to after I graduated high school and was old enough to DJ other places. I went from DJing random house parties and school dances to DJing low key lounges, cafes, and the occasional club. Lounges were cool, and I liked DJing lounge spots the best. Clubs, not so much. I quickly learned that he club scene wasn't really how I wanted to spend my DJ career. I didn't want to play radio hits and top 40 records or cater to terrible song requests from self-appointed drunk music experts on the dance floor. Nope! I wanted to play Hip Hop records like the DJs on the world famous Wake Up Show, or play records like the DJs I listened to on college radio stations at the time. So in 1996 I finally made the transition from club/lounge DJ to college radio DJ, where I could play anything I wanted to play without being hassled or harassed by drunks. For the first time I really felt at home.

College radio was also the place where I learned to always stay on top of the hard-to-find promos and independent releases. You really had to have records nobody else had, or records that most DJs couldn't easily get. You wanted to set yourself and your show apart from the other DJs on the air. That was just the environment we were in. The competition to break a record first was fierce on college radio. I tried to stay on my toes when it came to obtaining the hard to find records, which is really how I ended up collecting instrumental LPs. My first major instrumental LP was a promo copy of Bahamadia's debut album. I thought that this was something most people DJing wouldn't have, and I was right. Nobody I knew had a clue that this particular record even existed at the time, and nobody was really checking for records like these, either. My thing was to play instrumentals you couldn't find on 12" or anywhere else during my mic breaks or during on-air interviews with special guests. I became a fanatic for beats and collected a lot of instrumental LPs. All of the records you'll find in this book are instrumental records I've tracked down, discovered and collected over the years. You might ask why instrumental records? Well, because I think making beats is an underappreciated art form. We always celebrate the MC, but never the producers behind the music. If you think about the countless hours they spend searching through stacks and stacks of wax just for that perfect sound, sometimes only using a vintage machine with just ten seconds of sample time, you might appreciate what these producers do a lot more. Not to mention the blood, sweat, tears and hard work it takes to craft flawless beats from old dusty records like assembling a jigsaw puzzle. These records and the beats found between their grooves are the result of someone's dedication and passion, and I think it's about time to give them some shine. In essence, "Beats To The Rhyme" is more than just a book about collecting records and avoiding bootlegs; it's also about the appreciation of serious beats. Enjoy.

In this section, we'll focus on some of the instrumental records that were released commercially to stores and online retailers. Some of these releases are more scarce than others, but all were available for sale at one point in time. Most of the albums or records featured in this book either had a full length vocal predecessor or feature beats used at some point in a song, album, or single with vocals. Enjoy.

Artist: Aceyalone
Title: "Book Of Human Language" Instrumentals
Format: 2LP
Producer: Mumbles
Label: Mums The Word
Year: 2001
Cat#: Mum-01

Privately pressed and released by Mumbles in 2001 on his Mums The Word label, this record features all the beats he produced for Aceyalone's "Book Of Human Language" LP. You'll find this first pressing with the aqua blue label, and there are at least two other pressings that were released after this one. On a side note, the earliest version of this record was a white label promo pressing on Nu Gruv Alliance back in 1998. You'll find more info on that one in our Promo/Show vinyl section of the book.

Artist: Akbar
Title: "Big Bang Boogie" Instrumentals
Format: 2LP
Producers: M-Boogie, DJ Revolution, Thes One, This Kid Named Miles
Label: Ill Boogie
Year: 2001
Cat#: ILL72040

Akbar, frontman for the group The Mental Giants, released a solo album in 2001 on Ill Boogie records. As you can see by the names in the production section, this featured some familiar and respected names in the field of crafting beats. It's not particulary rare, but it's definitely worth tracking down for the music. This record comes in a plain white sleeve.

Artist: The Alchemist
Title: "Gangster Theme Music"
Format: LP
Producer: Alchemist
Label: ALC
Year: 2000
Cat#: ALC-001

Made to look like a library record release from the legendary KPM label, this one features beats previously used on other recordings produced by The Alchemist. It's basically a compilation of released and unreleased instrumentals appropriately titled "Gangster Theme Music" for the rugged street-style beats.

Artist: The Alchemist
Title: "Action/Drama" Instrumentals
Format: LP
Producer: Alchemist
Label: ALC
Year: 2001
Cat#: ALC-002

The second in the series of "The Chemistry Files" albums from The Alchemist was also made to look like an old library record. This time the theme is Action/Drama, with a nice selection of sinister street-style beats used in various recordings.

Artist: The Alchemist
Title: "Rapper's Best Friend" Instrumentals
Format: 2LP
Producer: Alchemist
Label: ALC/Decon
Year: 2007
Cat#: DCN-48-DLP

This is one of my favorite records in The Alchemist's instrumental series. It's comprised of previously unreleased beats and current studio material used for artists like Dilated Peoples, Mobb Deep and others. The cover art was inspired by the classic animated School House Rock shorts we used to watch as youngsters on Saturday mornings.

Artist: The Alchemist
Title: "1st Infantry" Instrumentals
Format: 2LP
Producer: Alchemist
Label: Koch
Year: 2005
Cat#: KOC-LP-9968

The instrumental companion to the "1st Infantry" LP offers all the beats found on the vocal LP. Here you'll find beats like "Hold You Down," featuring Nina Sky and Prodigy of Mobb Deep. This album's fairly common, but it's a solid addition to any collection.

Artist: The Alchemist
Title: "Rappers Best Friend Pt. 2" Instrumentals
Format: 2LP
Producer: Alchemist
Label: Decon
Year: 2012 Cat#: DCN-LP-151

Here's the second LP in the "Rappers Best Friend" series released by The Alchemist. It uses the same School House Rock-inspired artwork for the cover, and features more instrumental tracks that were previously unreleased or unavailable anywhere else. The album comes in a gatefold cover.

Artist: Aloe Blacc
Title: "Shine Through" Instrumentals
Format: 2LP
Producers: Aloe Blacc, Madlib, Oh No
Label: Stones Throw
Year: 2006
Cat#: STH2141

This record was released long before Aloe Blacc was known for his hit "I Need A Dollar." Before that, he was a talented MC and producer who released a number of Hip Hop records. This one on Stones Throw offers an eclectic selection of beats. The album comes in a generic white sleeve.

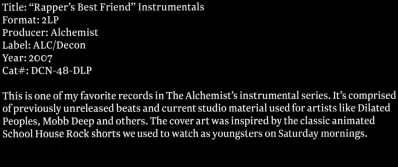

Artist: Al Tariq
Title: "God Connection" Instrumentals
Format: EP
Producers: The Beatnuts, No ID
Label: Correct
Year: 1997
Cat#: 10216

Correct was a promising Hip Hop label back in the mid to late 1990s, releasing a small number of high quality records before they folded. Al Tariq's "God Connection" LP was one of their best releases in my opinion. Out of all the Correct Record releases, only two instrumental EPs ever materialized. This one featured a small selection of instrumentals from the LP, which is a shame given the level of production here by the Beatnuts and No I.D.. Record comes in a black Correct Records sleeve.

Artist: Amerigo Gazaway
Title: "Bizarre Tribe" Instrumentals
Format: LP
Producer: Amerigo Gazaway
Label: Gummy Soul
Year: 2013
Cat#: BTIN

Gummy Soul and Amerigo Gazaway were behind this well-received album involving reconstructed and reworked beats inspired by A Tribe Called Quest, under a capellas from The Pharcyde. On this release you'll find just the instrumental tracks from the original record. There's also a special limited edition color vinyl version featuring the original LP and an instrumental disc. Record comes in a generic black sleeve.

Artist: Arsonists
Title: "As The World Burns" Instrumentals
Format: 2LP
Producers: Freestyle, D Stroy, Q-Unique
Label: Matador
Year: 1999
Cat#: OLE 419-1

Fondle Em introduced me to the Arsonists back in 1996 with their release of the "Session" 12-inch, which was an instant classic. If you're familiar with that single and enjoyed their production, you're gonna like the beats on the instrumental version. The record comes in a white sleeve with a sticker in the top left hand corner listing track information.

Artist: Asheru & Blue Black
Title: "Soon Come" Instrumentals
Format: 2LP
Producers: J Rawls, 88 Keys, Sound Providers, Yusef Dinero
Label: Seven Heads
Year: 2002
Cat#: SVH015

The Unspoken Heard released a number of rock-solid records in the mid to late 90s before their debut album, "Soon Come," finally materialized. The instrumental version soon followed and featured all the beautifully crafted beats by producers J Rawls, 88 Keys, Yusef Dinero and the Sound Providers. Album comes in a picture sleeve.

Artist: Boogie Down Productions
Title: "Criminal Minded" Instrumentals
Format: LP
Producers: BDP
Label: B Boy
Year: 1987, 1997
Cat#: BB5787

I've seen a number of different pressings for this instrumental LP. There are a couple of pressings with the normal "Criminal Minded" cover, and there's at least a few pressings with the yellow picture sleeve with Scott La Rock and KRS-One on the front. I've seen gold label versions, red label versions and this yellow label version. It's hard to keep up with them all. I believe this one is the more recent repress that came out in 1997. Luckily, I found it in the dollar bin. This record comes in the yellow club version sleeve with KRS-One and Scott La Rock on the cover.

Artist: Da Beatminerz
Title: "Brace 4 Impak" Instrumentals
Format: 2LP
Producers: Mr. Walt, Evil Dee
Label: Rawkus
Year: 2001
Cat#: RWK-1219

Da Beatminerz are known for crafting dark, punchy beats on their vintage samplers, so expect that same signature sound to be all over this LP. My favorite beat on this album would have to be the Reggae Dancehall inspired track, "Extreme Situation." Album comes in a plain black sleeve with a sticker in the top righthand corner.

Artist: Da Beatminerz
Title: "Fully Loaded With Statik" Instrumentals
Format: 2LP
Producers: Evil Dee, Mr. Walt
Label: Copter
Year: 2005
Cat#: 01CPT1003

I don't remember seeing a lot of these LPs when they first came out. They were kind of hard to track down for some odd reason. The new picture sleeve including Evil Dee and Mr. Walt on the front cover is a nice touch compared to the original artwork found on the vocal LP.

Artist: The Beatnuts
Title: "Intoxicated Demons" Instrumentals
Format: LP
Producers: The Beatnuts
Label: White
Year: 1997
Cat#: ID-00213-1

I'm really not too sure where these records originated from, but I heard they were released by The Beatnuts as a private pressing. The sound quality and the vinyl are just too good to be a cheap bootleg in my opinion. These are full length instrumentals from the original vocal tracks; they're not loops. Plus there's some unreleased material on these. The record comes in a white sleeve with a sticker in the middle of the cover. I'm always surprised by how easy to find and inexpensive this record is.

Artist: The Beatnuts
Title: "Street Level Vol. 1" Instrumentals
Format: LP
Producers: The Beatnuts
Label: White
Year: 1997
Cat#: SL-00211-1

Again, not really sure where these records originated from, but they all came out around the same time. I think I purchased Vol. 1 & 2 on the same day and later stumbled upon the "Intoxicated Demons" version. Here you'll find a collection of instrumentals from the Beatnuts' debut full length LP. More unreleased tracks can be found on this record, making this volume essential for any collection. Once again the vinyl quality and the mastering is excellent. The record comes in a white sleeve with a sticker in the middle of the cover.

Artist: The Beatnuts
Title: "Street Level Vol. 2" Instrumentals
Format: LP
Producers: The Beatnuts
Label: White
Year: 1997
Cat#: SL-00212-2

This is the last release in the series of early unreleased Beatnuts instrumentals. It contains the same excellent sound and vinyl quality as the first two records and also features 4 previously unreleased tracks from the vaults. These were probably songs that were just left off the album due to sample clearance issues. The instrumental "17" is really nice. Record comes in a black sleeve with a white sticker pasted in the middle.

Artist: The Beatnuts
Title: "Stone Crazy" Instrumentals
Format: LP
Producers: The Beatnuts
Label: White
Year: 1997
Cat#: DT-007

Origin is unknown, but it was released right after their "Stone Crazy" album came out. This record seems to have been pressed at the same plant as the other three Beatnuts instrumental records. The sound quality is also excellent. The record comes in a plain white sleeve with a sticker located in the top right hand corner. I've seen some cheap quality bootlegs of this one floating around without the sticker in the corner.

Artist: Blackalicious
Title: "Melodica" Instrumentals
Format: 2LP
Producers: Chief Xcel, DJ Shadow
Label: Mo Wax
Year: 1994
Cat#: MWSSLP-001

I found a brand new copy of this record back in 1995, but regrettably passed on it because of the $20 import price tag. Twenty bucks for an album back then was really expensive. After that day, I didn't see another copy until 2012! This pressing is dope, too, because it has the full cover artwork absent from the repress, which only had a sticker on the front cover. It also has the instrumentals that were missing from the domestic single vinyl pressing released by Sole Sides.

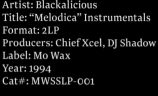

Artist: Blackalicious
Title: "Melodica" Instrumentals
Format: 2LP
Producers: Chief Xcel, DJ Shadow
Label: Mo Wax
Year: 1994
Cat#: MWSSLP-001

Here's what the label looks like on the second pressing from Mo Wax. It's way more common than the first pressing with the picture sleeve. It includes the same 2EP pressing with the bonus instrumental disc. Again, there's much more on the 2EP pressings compared to the much quieter single vinyl U.S. pressing on Sole Sides Records. It's a no-brainer if you ask me.

Artist: Black Milk
Title: "Popular Demand" Instrumentals
Format: 2LP
Producers: Black Milk
Label: Fat Beats
Year: 2007
Cat#: FB5112

This album comes with two discs. You'll find an instrumental version to Black Milk's "Popular Demand" LP and an instrumental version of his "Broken Wax" EP. Album comes in a double-sided picture sleeve.

Artist: Black Milk
Title: "Broken Wax" Instrumentals
Format: EP
Producers: Black Milk
Label: Fat Beats
Year: 2007
Cat#: FB5112

Here's what side D of Black Milk's "Popular Demand" instrumentals looks like. Here you'll find the instrumentals for his earlier "Broken Wax" EP.

Artist: Black Milk
Title: "Black And Brown" Instrumentals
Format: LP
Producers: Black Milk
Label: Fat Beats
Year: 2011
Cat#: FB5153

This release is the instrumental version to the celebrated album where Black Milk produces the beats and Danny Brown holds the mic. Record comes in a picture sleeve.

Artist: Black Moon
Title: "Unreleased Beats Pt. 1" instrumentals
Format: EP
Producers: Da Beatminerz
Label: Wreck
Year: 1998
Cat#: WR-20320

At one point, someone paid over $500 for a copy of a scarce Rainbo test pressing from the Beatminerz featuring these same beats found on Vol. 1 & 2. I do know there's at least one unreleased beat on the original test pressing that you won't find on anything else. Maybe that beat alone justifies the five bills? I tell you, the record market can be funny sometimes. These records were mostly overlooked when they first came out in 1998 and still aren't in very high demand in 2013. Here you'll find that golden era Beatminerz production that everyone loves. Record comes in a black sleeve with a sticker pasted across the top.

Artist: Black Moon
Title: "Unreleased Beats Pt. 2" instrumentals
Format: EP
Producers: Da Beatminerz
Label: Wreck
Year: 1998
Cat#: WR-20321

Part 2 features more unreleased beats from the classic debut album by Black Moon. You gotta have these two records right here. This one comes in a black sleeve with a sticker across the top.

Artist: Black Star
Title: "Black Star" Instrumentals
Format: LP
Producers: Hi Tek, Mr. Walt, Shawn J Period, J Rawls, 88 Keys
Label: Rawkus
Year: 1998

One of the more solid and consistent albums in the Rawkus catalogue gets the instrumental treatment. Check out the lineup of producers who worked on this record. Some of the best and most prolific producers at the time loaned their production skills for this album. Record comes in a generic black sleeve with a sticker in the top right hand corner.

Artist: Blaq Poet
Title: "Tha Blaqprint" Instrumentals
Format: LP
Producer: DJ Premier
Label: Year Round
Year: 2009
Cat#: YRR-2009INST

DJ Premier is considered to be the G.O.A.T. and a pioneer in the world of Hip Hop production. I don't know of another producer out there (besides Pete Rock or maybe Dilla) who has influenced the sound of more producers than Premier. Instrumental LPs produced entirely by Premier aren't something you see every day, either— I can think of only two other commercially released instrumental albums by him. All the other LPs from him are rare, private show vinyl pressings which usually fetch a lot at auction. Album comes in a picture sleeve.

Artist: Brother Ali
Title: "The Truth Is Here" Instrumentals
Format: 2LP
Producer: Ant
Label: Rhymesayers
Year: 2009
Cat#: RSE0104-1

Brother Ali and Rhymesayers released this limited edition EP back in 2009 that also came with a download card and a bonus instrumental disc. The instrumental disc has some really nice production on it from producer Ant, of Atmosphere. This record comes in a picture sleeve.

Artist: Bumpy Knuckles
Title: "Kolexxxion" Instrumentals
Format: 2LP
Producers: DJ Premier, Freddie Foxxx
Label: Gracie Productions/Works Of Mart
Year: 2012
Cat#: GCE-0008-1

I liked this record so much I bought two copies. It's a limited edition instrumental release with at least one exclusive bonus vocal track. The album comes in a picture sleeve with a new version of the original artwork, with DJ Premier solo on the front cover.

Artist: Cali Agents
Title: "Head Of The State" Instrumentals
Format: 2LP
Producers: Architect, Vin Roc, Brisk One, Richness, Camp Superflexxx
Label: Pockets Linted
Year: 2004
Cat#: PLE7023

The first Cali Agents album had incredible production, which kind of makes me wish they also pressed an instrumental disc for that one as well. Vin Roc produced some of the stronger highlights on this sophomore release. Record comes in a picture sleeve.

Artist: Celph Titled & Buckwild
Title: "Nineteen Ninety Now" Instrumentals
Format: 2LP
Producer: Buckwild
Label: No Sleep/Fat Beats
Year: 2011
Cat#: NSR007

The concept behind this record was to take unreleased beats Buckwild produced and recorded in the '90s and make a new album with that golden era sound. This resulted in a damn good instrumental album. Buckwild was a beast in the '90s on production, which is why I love this record. Here, you get all the instrumentals from the original vocal LP, plus four bonus beats unavailable on the original release. Win, win! The record comes in a picture sleeve.

Artist: Various
Title: "Chrome Children" Instrumentals
Format: 2LP
Producers: Madlib, J Dilla, Koushik, Aloe Blacc, J Roc, PB Wolf, Georgia Anne Muldrow, James Pants, J Rose
Label: Stones Throw
Year: 2007
Cat#: STH2152

This album was released in conjunction with Adult Swim network, which makes sense given the utter weirdness of this record. If you've ever watched Adult Swim on a late night you're already familiar with their use of Hip Hop beats in their broadcasts. Flying Lotus and MF Doom are a couple of their well-known contributors. That said, there's a lot to choose from on this record. My personal favorite would have to be the "Monkey Suite" instrumental produced by Madlib. Album comes in a plain white sleeve.

Artist: Common Sense
Title: "Resurrection" Instrumentals
Format: 2LP
Producers: No I.D., Ynot
Label: White
Year: 200?
Cat#: CMN-000

You'll see a number of bootlegs for this one as well. The first bootleg to surface looked like an official test pressing, but the vinyl quality was horrible and the sound was muddy. This one could be the third version I've come across and definitely the best sounding one. You'll also find a couple of short interludes on here that weren't found on other bootlegs. The vinyl is clean, the labels are printed clearly, and the sound quality is nice. Record comes in a plain white sleeve.

Artist: Common
Title: "Like Water For Chocolate" Instrumentals
Format: 2LP
Producers: DJ Premier, Jay Dee, Soulquarians, Questlove
Label: MCA
Year: 2000
Cat#: 088 112 437-1

MCA released this album in 2000 as a limited edition instrumental LP. Exactly how limited is up for debate, but it doesn't hold any bearing on the great quality of the record. The record offers a heavy selection of beats from producers J Dilla, Premier and Questlove. "Nag Champa" alone could bring a tear to your eye. The record comes in a black sleeve with a green sticker across the top.

Artist: Common
Title: "Be" Instrumentals
Format: 2LP
Producers: Jay Dee, Kanye West
Label: Good/Geffen
Year: 2005
Cat#: B0005032-01

The majority of this limited edition record is produced by Kanye West, but the late Jay Dee (J Dilla) also produced a couple of really brilliant tracks for this record. The album comes in a Good Records sleeve with an orange sticker across the top. I've seen a couple of bootlegs for this one as well.

Artist: The Creators
Title: "The Weight" Instrumentals
Format: 2LP
Producers: The Creators
Label: Bad Magic
Year: 2000
Cat#: MAGICLP2X

I think I received a couple of Creator records from the record pool I was in years ago that I liked, so I got into the Creators stuff for a little while. Back then the main records being promoted from the UK were from production teams like The Creators, The Nextmen and the Unsung Heroes. All of them had solid releases, but in the end their records remained largely unappreciated. I love the beats on this record. This album comes in a plain black sleeve with a bright red sticker in the top right hand corner.

Artist: Cypress Hill
Title: "Cypress Hill" Instrumentals
Format: LP
Producer: DJ Muggs
Label: White
Year: 2003
Cat#: 8305-Chill-1

I was told by a credible source that this record was pressed and released by DJ Muggs. It's definitely possible given the quality of this release. The record contains the full-length instrumentals to Cypress Hill's critically acclaimed debut album. It's basically the soundtrack to my early high school years. Record comes in a generic white sleeve.

Artist: Damu The Fudgemunk
Title: "When Winter Comes" Instrumentals
Format: 7"
Producer: Damu The Fudgemunk
Label: Redef
Year: 2011
Cat#: RDF-i701

The 7" single for this record featuring BUFF1 was first released on DWG/Redef as a limited edition pressing on both black and blue vinyl pressings. There were two vocal tracks featured on that first single, and the instrumentals were not included. Instead, Redef later released the 7" as an instrumental version pressed on blue vinyl. They also did a very small run of splatter pressings that I unfortunately missed out on. Good luck finding one of those.

Artist: Damu The Fudgemunk
Title: "Union Remixes" Instrumentals
Format: 10" EP
Producer: Damu The Fudgemunk
Label: Redef
Year: 2012
Cat#: RDF026

Damu The Fudgemunk provided a handful of standout remixes for a group called Union on a few of their record releases. Unfortunately, those Union records pressed on fancy colored vinyl didn't include the instrumental tracks, which were in high demand. Redef later released those instrumentals on this limited 10" single on both black and clear pressings. The clear pressing of course was the more limited version. Record comes in picture sleeve.

Artist: Dan The Automator
Title: "2K7" Instrumentals
Format: 2LP
Producer: The Automator
Label: Decon
Year: 2006
Cat#: DCN45DLP

I'm proud to say I haven't owned a video game system since Playstation 1, so I couldn't tell you much about 2K7. Apparently it's an NBA basketball game that The Automator was commissioned to provide the soundtrack for. This is the instrumental version to that soundtrack, which featured a bunch of artists like E40, A Tribe Called Quest, Hieroglyphics, Zion I among others. Record comes in picture sleeve.

Artist: Declaime
Title: "Illmimdmuzik" Instrumentals
Format: 2EP
Producer: Madlib
Label: Goodvibe
Year: 1999
Cat#: GVR2008-1

I think this record had a picture sleeve when it was released, but when I found my copy it was in a plain black sleeve and was missing the vocal disc. This one is an early Declaime release before all the Stones Throw stuff. The beats are what you'd expect in a record entirely produced by Madlib.

Artist: Declaime
Title: "Andsoitisaid" Instrumentals
Format: 2LP
Producers: Kankick, Madlib, Oh No
Label: Grooveattack
Year: 2001
Cat#: GAP081i

The line up of producers alone makes this record a great one to own. Anything with Kankick is a gem, really. Record comes in plain white sleeve.

Artist: De La Soul
Title: "AOI Mosaic Thump" Instrumentals
Format: 2LP
Producers: De La Soul, Supa Dave West, Ad Lib, Deaf 2 U, Rockwilder, Mr. Khaliyl
Label: Tommy Boy
Year: 2000
Cat#: TB1437

I remember this one being a promo-only pressing in the beginning, which is why I first paid a premium "promo only" price for my first copy. But later on, Tommy Boy finally distributed these to retailers as an official De La Soul release. If you look on the back cover of the commercial version, you'll notice that Tommy Boy just put bar code stickers over the phrase "For Promotional Use Only" printed on the back of the original covers. Album comes in a blue picture sleeve.

Artist: De La Soul
Title: "AOI: Bionix" Instrumentals
Format: 2LP
Producers: Pos, Kev Brown, Megahertz, Jay Dee, Deaf 2 U, Jose Hernandez
Label: Tommy Boy
Year: 2000
Cat#: TB1546

Now every time I hear Paul McCartney's, "Wonderful Christmas" I think of this De La Soul record. They used the sample for the cut "Simply" here and it's one of the highlights of the record. Album comes in picture sleeve.

Artist: The Demigodz
Title: "The Gods Must Be Crazy" Instrumentals
Format: 2EP
Producers: Apathy, Celph Titled, JJ Brown
Label: Ill Boogie
Year: 2002
Cat#: ILL72052-1

This particular Demigodz EP was part of the Earplug series released by Ill Boogie records. All of the Earplug releases came with a bonus instrumental disc, which was really the best part for me. The production on these records were always top notch. EP comes in a green picture sleeve.

Artist: Deltron
Title: "Deltron 3030" Instrumentals
Format: 2LP
Producer: Dan The Automator
Label: 75Ark
Year: 2001
Cat#: 75004

This record, featuring Del The Funky Homosapien as his alter ego Deltron, is something of a cult classic and considered by many to be Del's best work. I'll leave that up for debate. Album is produced entirely by Dan The Automator and comes in a picture sleeve. The cover art on this instrumental version is basically the same as the artwork found on the vocal LP, only it's blue and you'll notice the people standing on the catwalk from the original cover are missing on this LP.

Artist: Diamond D
Title: "B Sides & Bootlegs" Instrumentals
Format: LP
Producer: Diamond D
Label: Dusty Fingers
Year: 2001
Cat#: DF444

This particular record offers some harder to find instrumentals and unreleased material from Diamond D, like the 45 King remix for "Best Kept Secret," which was originally only available on a rare promo pressing. You'll also find some bonus beats and instrumentals like "Build Ya Skillz" that he produced for KRS-One, which is only available on this record. The album comes in a white sleeve with a sticker across the top.

Artist: Diamond D
Title: "Stunts, Blunts, & Hip Hop" Instrumentals
Format: 2LP
Producer: Diamond D
Label: none
Year: 1998
Cat#: DF222

The vocal version for this album still fetches around $100 to $150 to this day. For some strange reason you can still find a copy of the instrumentals released for this Diamond D classic on his Dusty Fingers imprint for less than twenty bucks. Album comes in a white cover with a sticker across the top. You can't front on that.

Artist: Dilated Peoples
Title: "The Platform" Instrumentals
Format: 2LP
Producers: Evidence, Kut Masta Kurt, E Swift, DJ Babu, T-Ray
Label: ABB
Year: 2000
Cat#: ABB1017

I think I got this record from the ABB offices in Oakland. It came in a generic black cover, so I pasted a Dialated Peoples logo sticker in the top right hand corner of my personal copy. Man, I miss those days at the ABB offices. This would be the first pressing with the brown label. The second pressing had a white label with "Instrumentals" after the album title.

Artist: Dilated Peoples
Title: "Neighborhood Watch" Instrumentals
Format: 2LP
Producers: Evidence, Babu, Alchemist, Joey Chavez
Label: ABB
Year: 2004
Cat#: ABB1060-1

I wouldn't say this was one of my favorite Dilated Peoples album of all time, but there are some nice beats on there, like the lead single, "Marathon." Album comes in a generic white sleeve with a sticker across the top.

Artist: Diverse
Title: "One A.M." Instrumentals
Format: 2LP
Producers: RJD2, Madlib, Prefuse 73, Overflo, Jeff Parker
Label: Chocolate Industries
Year: 2004
Cat#: CSP-001

Apparently this album was a limited release of 2,000 copies pressed worldwide, but it's fairly common to find sealed copies today for less than $20. Album comes in a generic white sleeve with a blue sticker across the top.

Artist: Dr. Dooom
Title: "First Come, First Served" Instrumentals
Format: 2LP
Producer: Kut Masta Kurt
Label: Funky Ass
Year: 1999
Cat#: KTR-010A

It was impossible to keep up with the flurry of Kool Keith related record releases on labels like Funky Ass, Mo Wax, Bulk and Threshold recordings. And unfortunately only a small number of those quirky albums had an instrumental pressing, like this weird horror core album under the pseudonym Dr. Dooom. The production on this record is rugged, quirky, moody and a little eerie, like an old childrens Halloween record. The track "Apt 223" on this LP also appeared in the film "Grandma's Boy." Record comes in a black sleeve with a sticker in the top left hand corner.

Artist: Dr. Dre
Title: "The Chronic 2001" Instrumentals
Format: 2LP
Producers: Dr. Dre, Mel Man, Lord Finesse
Label: Aftermath/Interscope
Year: 1999
Cat#: 069490572

Dr. Dre is another producer considered by many hardcore Hip Hop fans to be the greatest of all time when it comes to making beats. Here you'll find all the instrumentals for his critically acclaimed "Chronic 2001" LP, released back in 1999. My favorite cut and the instrumental I find myself playing the most is "The Message," produced by Lord Finesse. Record comes in a plain black sleeve with a sticker in the top right hand corner.

Artist: Dr. No
Title: "Tornado Funk" Instrumentals
Format: LP
Producer: Oh No
Label: FiveDayWeekend
Year: 2012
Cat#: FDW-7715

I prefer this record over the "Ohnomite" release because of the overall cohesiveness of this record compared to the vocal version. As an instrumental record this record just makes more sense to me. Here, you'll find instrumentals and alternate mixes from The "Ohnomite" album , which draws samples from the Dolomite films and music. The record comes in a picture sleeve.

Artist: Dr. Octagon
Title: "Instrumentalyst (Octagon Beats)"
Format: 2LP
Producer: Dan the Automator
Label: Mo Wax
Year: 1996
Cat#: MW064LP

"Dr. Octagonecologist" was really the beginning of Kool Keith's illustrious oddball career. Songs like "Blue Flowers," "Earth People," "3000" and "Halfsharkalligator Halfman" were just a few of his unorthodox cult hits. If the vocals were a little much for you, you could get down with the instrumentals, found here on "Instrumentalyst (Octagon Beats)." There are two pressings for this record. This first pressing is on Mo Wax and the second one is pressed domestically on Bulk Recordings. The cover for this record has a skeleton arm on the front.

Artist: Dr. Octagon
Title: "Dr. Octagon" Instrumentals
Format: 2LP
Producer: Dan the Automator
Label: Bulk
Year: 1997
Cat#: MW064LP

Here's the version released domestically on Bulk Recordings. This one came in either a plain black cover or a plain white cover with a sticker in the top right hand corner. The Bulk Recording versions have solid green labels. It was also available on CD for those who weren't into vinyl.

Artist: Dudley Perkins
Title: "A Lil Light" Instrumentals
Format: 2LP
Producer: Madlib
Label: Stones Throw
Year: 2003
Cat#: STH2074

Vocally, "A Lil Light" was very soulful and lyrically deep. It was unlike any other Hip Hop release at the time. Madlib's production reflected Dudley's lyrical poetry and raw emotion on the record. This is one of Stones Throw's best records in my opinion. Album comes in a generic black sleeve.

Artist: Dudley Perkins
Title: "Expressions" Instrumentals
Format: 2LP
Producer: Madlib
Label: Stones Throw
Year: 2006
Cat#: STH2140

Dudley's second album released on Stones Throw was also produced by Madlib. You'll find the beats on this one to be highly influenced by Jazz, Funk and Soul. The record comes in a generic white sleeve.

Artist: Dynas
Title: "The Apartment" Instrumentals
Format: 2EP
Producers: DJ Jazzy Jeff, DJ Spinna, J Dilla, Illastrate, DJ Rhettmatic
Label: BBE
Year: 2009
Cat#: BBE151ALP

Overall, this is a very solid EP release from the Dynas. Every contributing producer who worked on this record brought something beautiful to the table, especially J Dilla on the title cut for this record, "The Apartment." The beat is just incredible. This record comes in a picture sleeve with the instrumentals on disc two.

Artist: Various
Title: "Eastern Conference Greatest Vol. 1" Instrumentals
Format: 2LP
Producers: RJD2, Alchemist, Mighty Mi, J Zone, Reef, V.I.C
Label: Eastern Conference
Year: 2005
Cat#: ECR1018

This right here is a compilation of beats taken from various Eastern Conference related releases. You'll find some unreleased material on here as well, which is always a huge plus. Eastern Conference was a strong label in the late nineties and early 2000s era, so everything on this record is solid. The album comes in a plain white sleeve with a sticker across the top.

Artist: DJ Eclipse
Title: "DJ Eclipse Remixes Circa 1994" Instrumentals
Format: LP
Producer: DJ Eclipse
Label: Eclipse/Fatbeats
Year: 2004
Cat#: ECL-2004

I was fortunate enough to find a promo copy of this record with only a plain white sleeve and a gold promo stamp in one of the corners. The regular release (if you ever come across one) had a green picture sleeve. Here you'll find a bunch of previously unreleased and highly sought after remixes produced by DJ Eclipse, including the coveted Eclipse remix for OC's "Born 2 Live," which was only available as a test pressing from Wild Pitch. This record includes the vocal and instrumental tracks on two discs.

Artist: Ed OG
Title: "My Own Worst Enemy" Instrumentals
Format: 2LP
Producers: Pete Rock, Diamond D, DJ Supreme One, DJ Revolution
Label: Fat Beats
Year: 2004
Cat#: FB5112INSTR

Almost entirely produced by Pete Rock, "My Own Worst Enemy" is loaded with dusty beats, thick bass lines and crisp drum programming. Diamond D makes an appearance on production here which is also a big plus. This record comes in a plain black sleeve.

Artist : El Da Sensei
Title: "Relax, Relate, Release" Instrumentals
Format: 2LP
Producers: Da Boy Wonder, DJ Kaos, J Rawls, Kankick, Koolade, Malito, P Original, Sebb
Label: Seven Heads
Year: 2002
Cat#: SVH-32

A whole lot of talented producers worked on this record, including Kankick, J Rawls, and P Original, just to name a few. The entire record is rock solid. The album comes in a picture sleeve.

Artist: Emanon
Title: "On and On" Instrumentals
Format: 2EP
Producers: Aloe Blacc, Exile, DJ Cheapshot
Label: Ill Boogie
Year: 2002
Cat#: ILL72055-1

This record release was part of the short-lived Earplug series on the Ill Boogie label, which featured early production from Aloe Blacc and Exile. These records were always a two-disc set that included vocal tracks and instrumentals. All the Earplug records had very similar artwork for the cover designs.

Artist: Evidence
Title: "Yellow Tape" Instrumentals
Format: 2LP
Producer: Evidence
Label: Battle Axe
Year: 2003
Cat#: BAX1030

The "Yellow Tape" LP was the first in a two-part series of compilation albums featuring instrumentals produced by Evidence of Dilated Peoples. Some of the beats offered here were also unreleased. The album comes in a picture sleeve.

Artist: Evidence
Title: "Red Tape" Instrumentals
Format: 2LP
Producer: Evidence
Label: Decon
Year: 2007
Cat#: DCN51DLP

This is part two of the "Tape" compilations, featuring more instrumentals and unreleased beats produced by Evidence of Dilated Peoples. The cover art is also the same as "Yellow Tape," only this time the evidence tape blocking the evidence room is red. These were also available on CD.

Artist: Fat Jack
Title: "Cater To The DJ" Instrumentals
Format: LP
Producer: Fat Jack
Label: Celestial
Year: 2000
Cat#: CSL82006-1

The vocal version of this record was a huge stack of four LPs, and featured almost thirty tracks with guest appearances by some of Fat Jack's Project Blowed cohorts. With only seven tracks on this record, this one is more like an album sampler. There's some dope beats on here, though, and it's definitely worth tracking down. This record comes in a black sleeve with a blue sticker across the top.

Artist: Five Deez
Title: "Koolmotor" Instrumentals
Format: 2LP
Producer: Fat Jon
Label: Counterflow
Year: 2001
Cat#: CF016-1

There aren't many producers out there than can do what Fat Jon is capable of doing with a sampler. His beats can be very complex and change direction on you, or be beautifully simple and straight forward. He's definitely a master of his craft, and in my opinion is highly underappreciated. The instrumental version to the Five Deez "Koolmotor" album is just brilliant. This album comes in a picture sleeve.

Artist: Five Deez
Title: "Kinkynasti" Instrumentals
Format: 2LP
Producer: Fat Jon
Label: K7
Year: 2003
Cat#: K7151LP1

I can't really say enough about Fat Jon and his beats. The dude is a musical genius. The full length instrumental version to the Five Deez second album carries more brilliant production from the Ample Soul Physician. Check out "The Ocean," "Sextraterrestrial," "Hey Young World" or "Another Love Affair," just to name a few. The record comes in a black sleeve with a purple sticker across the top.

Artist: Five Deez
Title: "Kommunicator" Instrumentals
Format: 2LP
Producer: Fat Jon
Label: Ample Soul
Year: 2006
Cat#: AS243-1

The Five Deez third instrumental album was released on Fat Jon's Ample Soul label as a double LP. Overall this one is more electronically driven and soulful than any previous Five Deez albums. But the beats are still very much Hip Hop, and they're carried by punchy kicks and crisp snares behind synthesized sounds and dusty soundscapes. This record comes in a black picture sleeve.

Artist: The Foreign Exchange
Title: "Connected" Instrumentals
Format: 2LP
Producer: Nicolay
Label: BBE
Year: 2004
Cat#: BBELP1047

The name "The Foreign Exchange" came from the way this album was recorded. Nicolay, being from the Netherlands, would produce music electronically and send beats via email to Phonte of Little Brother, who lived here in the States. Phonte would then send the finished song back to Nicolay, back and forth, until the album was completed. The rest, as they say, is history. They've been successfully making music together ever since. The album comes with a picture sleeve.

Artist: Foreign Legion
Title: "Kidnappervan" Instrumentals
Format: 2LP
Producer: DJ Design
Label: Insidious Urban
Year: 2000
Cat#: IUR9000-1

I used to come across this record a lot when I was out looking for music. A lot of sealed copies, too, mostly priced under $5. Now I don't come across it very much at all. I guess people finally woke up and realized how good this record actually is. DJ Design had serious beats. Unfortunately for me, for some reason all of the instrumentals from the "Kidnappervan" LP aren't available on the instrumental version. I really would've liked to have them all, but it is what it is. This album comes in a generic black sleeve with a sticker across the top.

Artist: Frankenstein
Title: "UV" Instrumentals
Format: 2EP
Producer: Frankenstein
Label: Knowledge Of Self
Year: 1997
Cat#: KOSV-350

Frankenstein had a solid run during the mid to late '90s releasing a small number of high-quality releases on his Knowledge Of Self Label. This was probably his last release on Knowledge Of Self before he seemed to just vanish into obscurity. This EP comes with a vocal disc and a bonus instrumental record.

Artist: Freestyle Fellowship
Title: "Inner City Griots" Instrumentals
Format: 2LP
Producers: Earthquake Brothers, DJ Kiilu, Freestyle Fellowship, Mattmattiks
Label: Sub Level Epidemic
Year: 2002
Cat#: SLELP002

Licensed and released by Sub Level as a limited edition pressing on clear vinyl, this album comes in a picture sleeve and contains the instrumentals to the Freestyle Fellowship's debut album. It's supposed to be a rare release, but it isn't very rare, really— I still come across this one quite often.

Artist: Gagle
Title: "Big Bang Theory" Instrumentals
Format : 2LP
Producer: DJ Mitsu The Beats
Label: Jazzy Sport
Year: 2005
Cat#: JSV-012

Jazzy Sport, one of the more prolific Japanese labels, released this limited edition instrumental version of Gagle's "Big Bang Theory" LP. The only way to get this was from Japan, or possibly select online retailers in the UK if you were lucky enough to track one down. Album comes in a picture sleeve with the same artwork you see on the label.

Artist: Gagle
Title: "3Peat" Instrumentals
Format: 2LP
Producer: DJ Mitsu The Beats
Label: Jazzy Sport
Year: 2008
Cat#: JSV-502

Gagle's "3Peat" instrumental was another well produced album by DJ Mitsu The Beats. It was also another limited pressing from Jazzy Sport, which was only available across the water from Japan or Europe. A few copies slipped through customs and found their way into some US shops. I found my copy at a local shop in San Francisco. Album comes in a white picture sleeve. Most of the song titles are written in Japanese.

Artist: Gang Starr
Title: "The Ownerz" Instrumentals
Format: 3LP
Producer: DJ Premier
Label: Virgin
Year: 2003
Cat#: 7143-5-93749-1-8

I remember that when "The Ownerz" first came out most diehard fans didn't like it as much as the previous Gang Starrs LPs, but I thought it was a really solid record. Now that GURU has passed away I appreciate this album even more. Gang Starr will always be one of my favorite groups. This LP is a triple-disc set with a one-sided third disc. Album comes in a picture sleeve.

Artist: Georgia Anne Muldrow
Title: "Olesi: Fragments" Instrumentals
Format: LP
Producer: Georgia Anne Muldrow
Label: Stones Throw
Year: 2006
Cat#: STH2147

Georgia Anne Muldrow is one of the few female producers out there appreciated as a master producer. She's produced or created remixes for a long list of well-known artists, and she has beats for days. This is the instrumental version of her only album on Stones Throw. I would describe the beats as being heavily influenced by J Dilla. Record comes in a plain white sleeve.

Artist: Ghostface Killah
Title: "12 Reasons To Die" Instrumentals
Format: LP
Producer: Adrian Younge
Label: Soultemple
Year: 2013
Cat#: STE112

Ghostface Killah recently released a new album on the Soultemple label produced entirely by Adrian Younge, the man behind the funky music on the Black Dynamite soundtrack. The music sounds like a classic Wu Tang album recorded with live instrumentation. It's easily one of Ghostface Killah's best albums in recent years. Record comes in a picture sleeve with movie poster style artwork.

Artist: Godfather Don
Title: "Diabolique" Instrumentals
Format: 2LP
Producer: Godfather Don
Label: Hydra
Year: 1998
Cat#: HYD-801A

I found my copy of this album at the old Fat Beats music shop in LA by accident. I didn't even know it existed until I stumbled across it at the shop. It looks exactly like the vocal release, the only difference is that the cover on the instrumental version has a sticker across the top with "instrumentals" printed in red letters.

Artist: Grooveman Spot
Title: "Eternal Development" Instrumentals
Format: 2LP
Producer: Grooveman Spot
Label: Planetgroove
Year: 2007
Cat#: PGLP-P1004

The vocal version for this album features guest appearances by Grap Luva, Count Bass D and OC, among many others, and has a sound heavily influenced by J Dilla. This instrumental pressing also comes in the same picture sleeve as its vocal predecessor, but the color has been changed to red instead of the original green.

Artist: Grooveman Spot
Title: "Change Situations" Instrumentals
Format: LP
Producer: Grooveman Spot
Label: Planetgroove
Year: 2010
Cat#: PGLP-P 1008

Planetgroove/Jazzy Sport made limited white label promo pressings before that were available in retail shops, like this one for the Grooveman Spot instrumentals. Limited to 150 copies worldwide. You'll find some of these records with blank labels, while others will have stickers affixed to the label with track listings. Album also has a generic white sleeve.

Artist: GZA/Genius
Title: "Liquid Swords" Instrumentals
Format: 2LP
Producer: RZA
Label: Geffen/Getondown
Year: 2013
Cat#: GET-54055-LP

Eighteen years after the promo-only instrumental "Liquid Swords" LP, GetOnDown. com and Geffen Records finally released the instrumentals in a 4LP boxset for the 2013 Record Store Day edition. The limited edition boxset consisted of the 2LP vocal version, the 2LP instrumentals, a wooden chess set, stickers and a booklet with photos, lyrics and general info about the classic "Liquid Swords" LP. 750 copies were made.

Artist: Handsome Boy Modeling School
Title: "White People" Instrumentals
Format: 2LP
Producers: Dan The Automator, Prince Paul
Label: Atlantic
Year: 2004
Cat#: 62988-1

Handsome Boy Modeling School's second album continues the light-hearted humor found on "White People." Too bad the first album didn't have an instrumental pressing because the production on both records was top notch. Album comes in a picture sleeve with Nathanial Merriweather (Automator) and Chest Rockwell (Prince Paul) blacked out of the original artwork.

Artist: Hieroglyphics
Title: "Full Circle" Instrumentals
Format: 2LP
Producers: Opio, A Plus, Domino
Label: Hiero Imperium
Year: 2004
Cat#: 62988-1

Very few of Hieroglyphics' albums get the instrumental treatment. When I say few, I mean this is basically one of only two releases besides the "93 Til" instrumental LP that was commercially available to the general public. Album comes in a generic white sleeve .

Artist: The High & Mighty
Title: "Home Field Advantage" Instrumentals
Format: 2LP
Producers: DJ Mighty Mi, Alchemist, Reef
Label: Rawkus
Year: 1999
Cat#: RWK-1168-1

The High & Mighty scored some underground success in the late '90s with songs like "B-Boy Document," "Hands On Experience," "The Meaning," and "It's All For You" before signing with Rawkus and releasing their debut album in 1999. "Home Field Advantage" was one of my favorite records back then for the comedic lyrics and lush beats. Instrumental version comes in a black sleeve with a sticker in the top right hand corner.

Artist: House Shoes
Title: "Let It Go" Instrumentals
Format: 2LP
Producer: House Shoes
Label: Tres
Year: 2013
Cat#: TR396-087

Tres Records pressed this instrumental album in a limited run of only 500 copies, which may explain the higher than average retail price of $25 for these. Album also has the same cover artwork as the original vocal version, only this time it's toned down from red to black and white.

Artist: InI
Title: "Center Of Attention" Instrumentals
Format: LP
Producer: Pete Rock
Label: White
Year: 200
Cat#: 21322

Unfortunately, the original InI album was shelved by Elektra back in 1996. Since then, there have been a number of unofficial bootlegs floating around with different track listings, labels or covers. Most of these are incomplete albums with key tracks missing; then there are these with the black and white labels. The word on the street is that these were semi-official and pressed by someone involved with the group. You'll find full length instrumentals to a select number of songs off the legendary "Center Of Attention" album. Record comes in a generic white sleeve.

Artist: Jay Dee
Title: "Welcome To Detroit" Instrumentals
Format: 2LP
Producer: Jay Dee
Label: BBE
Year: 2005
Cat#: BBE-BG-LPI-001

BBE officially pressed these instrumentals four years after the original vocal album was released. This special instrumental version also carries the same cover design as the original LP. A limited edition "10th Anniversary" version offering an alternate cover also surfaced back in 2011.

Artist: Jay Dee
Title: "Jay Deelicious" Instrumentals
Format: 2LP
Producer: Jay Dee
Label: Delicious Vinyl
Year: 2007
Cat#: DV-9033

After J Dilla died the flood gates were blasted open, clearing the path for hundreds of compilations and tribute albums like this one, which was released by Delicious Vinyl in 2007. "Jay Deelicious" is a three record set pressed and repressed numerous times on a variety of colors. This pressing just happens to be blue, green and clear. You'll find a selection of remixes on here that Jay Dee produced during his Delicious Vinyl years. Instrumentals are also included with the vocal tracks. Album comes with a picture sleeve.

Artist: Jaylib
Title: "Champion Sound" Instrumentals
Format: 2LP
Producers: J Dilla, Madlib
Label: Stones Throw
Year: 2003
Cat#: STH-2079

The concept of this album resulted from a role reversal of sorts. The original vocal version has J Dilla rhyming over Madlib beats, while Madlib rhymes over J Dilla beats. The instrumental version soon followed. Album comes in a generic black sleeve.

Artist: DJ Jazzy Jeff
Title: "The Magnificent" Instrumentals
Format: 2LP
Producers: DJ Jazzy Jeff, Kev Brown, P Smoovah, Ken Wood
Label: BBE
Year: 2002
Cat#: LC07306

Here's a solid album featuring early Kev Brown production from when he was still a part of Jeff's A Touch Of Jazz production team. Album comes in a black sleeve with a white sticker pasted across the top.

Artist: J Dilla
Title: "The Shining" Instrumentals
Format: 2LP
Producer: J Dilla
Label: BBE
Year: 2006
Cat#: BBECD077

J Dilla's second album on the BBE label featured guest appearances by Common, Busta Rhymes, Black Thought and Guilty Simpson, among others. For me, the main focus of this record is the genius behind the beats. Album comes in a gatefold cover with Louis Vuitton inspired artwork.

Artist: J Dilla
Title: "Ruff Draft" Instrumentals
Format: LP
Producer: J Dilla
Label: Stones Throw
Year: 2007
Cat#: STH2159

I was handed a promo cassette of the "Ruff Draft" album one day while shopping for records in San Francisco. Originally the "Ruff Draft" cassettes came inside a box set with a Dilla tee shirt and a copy of the LP, if I'm not mistaken. Later the instrumentals surfaced with a generic black cover. A more recent pressing appeared after Stones Throw decided to repackage these instrumentals with a picture sleeve of the original artwork with the title, "Ruff Draft Beats," on the front cover.

Artist: J Dilla
Title: "Yancey Boys" Instrumentals
Format: 2LP
Producer: J Dilla
Label: Delicious Vinyl
Year: 2008
Cat#: DV9047-A

This album was a solid effort featuring singing and MCing over J Dilla beats, but the real essence of the "Yancey Boys" album for me is the production from Dilla. Album comes with full picture sleeve.

Artist: J Dilla
Title: "Yancey Boys" Instrumentals
Format: 2LP
Producer: J Dilla
Label: Delicious Vinyl
Year: 2013
Cat#: DV9047

This instrumental album featuring unreleased beats by the late J Dilla was originally released back in 2008 on regular black vinyl. Delicious Vinyl decided to reissue the record again in 2013 on this special white vinyl pressing for collectors and fans of Dilla's work. Album comes in the original picture sleeve.

Artist: J Dilla
Title: "Donut Shop" Instrumentals
Format: 2LP
Producer: J Dilla
Label: Stones Throw
Year: 2010
Cat#: STH2248

One of the more cleverly designed LPs from Stones Throw, this record comes packaged like a pink donut box gatefold cover. Open it up and illustrated donuts line the inner cover. This is a 2LP set featuring unreleased beats produced by J Dilla for artists like A Tribe Called Quest and Busta Rhymes. The set also includes two donut slip mats, and one side of each record has a Serato tone for use with the Serato DJ setup.

Artist: J Dilla
Title: "Rebirth Of Detroit" Instrumentals
Format: 2LP
Producer: J Dilla
Label: Ruff Draft
Year: 2013
Cat#: RD004

Instrumental version to the recent "Rebirth Of Detroit" album features previously unreleased beats by the late J Dilla. Album comes with picture sleeve.

Artist: Jehst
Title: "Falling Down" Instrumentals
Format: 2LP
Producers: Jehst, Lewis Parker, LG, Cee Why, Apollo,
Label: Low Life
Year: 2003
Cat#: LOW31LP

I used to follow Low Life Records mainly for the beats. All of their releases had really nice production, so I'd usually pick up the instrumental versions when I could. Imports like these from labels like Low Life weren't really available here in the States so you'd usually have to order online from their website. I happened to find a copy of Jehst's "Falling Down" instrumentals from a shop in Oregon somewhere. I love this record. It has a couple of early Lewis Parker beats on there too. Album comes in a black and white version of the original picture sleeve.

Artist: Jehst
Title: "Nuke Proof Suit" Instrumentals
Format: LP
Producer: Jehst
Label: High Plains
Year: 2005
Cat#: REPHP001Inst

This was another album I had to purchase from someone overseas. It's the instrumental version to Jehst's "Nuke Proof Suit" LP, which was unavailable here in the States. The beats are dope. Album comes in a blue hazmat suit inspired picture sleeve.

Artist: Jeru The Damaja
Title: "Divine Design" Instrumentals
Format: LP
Producers: Ed Dantez, Sabor
Label: Ashenafi
Year: 2003
Cat#: ASHE-0

Here's kind of a strange Jeru The Damaja instrumental release for an album I've never even heard of. It was manufactured and distributed by Caroline Distribution, which I don't think is in business anymore either. What can I say? The album is a far stretch from the beats we're accustomed to hearing Jeru on, like the beats for "The Sun Rises in the East" and "Wrath of the Math." But it's okay. If you're a Jeru completist, you might consider owning this one. Album comes in a plain black picture sleeve.

Artist: J Live
Title: "The Best Part" Instrumentals
Format: LP
Producers: DJ Premier, Pete Rock, Prince Paul, 88 Keys, Grap Luva, DJ Spinna
Label: Triple Threat
Year: 2002
Cat#: TTP007

Record label politics and circumstance played a huge role in why this album almost disappeared forever. In a nutshell, J Live had problems with his first label. He left that label and signed with another label. That new label's parent company was sold to another major corporation and the plug was pulled once again on "The Best Part." Years later bootleg copies of the album finally surfaced, but the official release ended up being pressed on Triple Threat, and the instrumental version soon followed. Record comes in a picture sleeve.

Artist: J Rawls
Title: "The Essence Of J Rawls" Instrumentals
Format: 2LP
Producer: J Rawls
Label: Grooveattack
Year: 2001
Cat#: GAP073i

You'll find the beats from J Rawls to be extra hefty awith a heavy Jazz influence on this one. It's definitely one of the best albums on the Grooveattack label for Jazzy Hip Hop if it's what you're into. Record comes in a plain white sleeve.

Artist: Jungle Brothers
Title: "Straight Out The Jungle" Instrumentals
Format: 2LP
Producers: Jungle Brothers
Label: Warlock/Traffic
Year: 2006
Cat#: TEG-75511

Traffic released this special edition instrumental LP for the Jungle Brothers debut album, which was originally a test pressing-only record used by their DJ on tours. Here you'll find all the instrumentals from the "Straight Out The Jungle" album with other bonus show beats. Record comes in a picture sleeve.

Artist: Jurassic 5
Title: "Quality Control" Instrumentals
Format: 2LP
Producers: Cut Chemist, DJ Nu-Mark
Label: Rawkus
Year: 2000
Cat#: RWK 1183

Hard to believe this album is thirteen years old now. We listened to this record the whole trip to Los Angeles and back one summer, it was that good. It was equally amazing seeing them live with Dialated Peoples. This instrumental version was most likely the same record played during their live shows, but I do remember seeing a test pressing for these instrumentals on Rainbo, which was probably the first pressing before Rawkus released them. Album comes in a picture sleeve with the members of Jurassic 5 removed from the original artwork.

Artist: Jurassic 5
Title: "Power In Numbers" Instrumentals
Format: 2LP
Producers: Cut Chemist, DJ Nu-Mark, JuJu, Sa Ra
Label: Up Above
Year: 2002
Cat#: UA 3039-1

Jurassic 5's second album carries much of the same energy and funky, sample heavy production "Quality Control" had. Songs like "What's Golden," "Freedom," and the brilliant cut "Day At The Races," with Big Daddy Kane and Percee P, appear on this album. Record comes with picture sleeve.

Artist: Jurassic 5
Title: "Feedback" Instrumentals
Format: 2LP
Producers: DJ Nu-Mark Salaam Remi
Label: Up Above
Year: 2006
Cat#: UPA3136-1

By this time Cut Chemist wasn't involved with the release, so the sound behind this particular album went in a much different direction than their previous work. There are still some nice cuts on here though. Album comes in picture sleeve.

Artist: J Zone
Title: "Music For Tu Madre" & "A Bottle Of Whup Ass" Instrumentals
Format: LP
Producer: J Zone
Label: Old Maid
Year: 1999
Cat#: OME-003

This one with the aqua blue label was the first pressing on Old Maid, and featured a selection of instrumentals from J Zone's first two LPs. Album comes in a plain white sleeve.

Artist: J Zone
Title: "Instrumentals Vol. 1" Instrumentals
Format: LP
Producer: J Zone
Label: Old Maid/Fat Beats
Year: 2002
Cat#: OME-2003

This one with the green label was the second pressing released by Fat Beats featuring instrumentals from "Music For Tu Madre" and "A Bottle Of Whup Ass." Same as the one with the aqua blue label released by J Zone on Old Maid. Record comes in plain white sleeve.

Artist: J Zone
Title: "Pimps Don't Pay Taxes" Instrumentals
Format: LP
Producer: J Zone
Label: Old Maid/Fat Beats
Year: 2001
Cat#: OME-2005

This pressing with the orange label features most of the beats found on J Zone's "Pimps Don't Pay Taxes" LP. Record comes in a plain white sleeve.

Artist: J Zone
Title: "The Lost Instrumentals" Instrumentals
Format: LP
Producer: J Zone
Label: Old Maid
Year: 2002
Cat#: OME-2007

This release with the silver label features instrumentals and beats from kits and interludes found on various J Zone albums. Record comes in a plain white sleeve.

Artist: J Zone
Title: "The Gold Plaque" Instrumentals
Format: LP
Producer: J Zone
Label: Old Maid
Year: 2003
Cat#: OME-2012

This one with the gold label offers beats from a variety of records produced by J Zone. You'll find instrumentals for artists like The High & Mighty, Cage, and J Zone himself, among others. Record comes in a plain white sleeve.

Artist: J Zone
Title: "The Pink Cookies" Instrumentals
Format: LP
Producer: J Zone
Label: Old Maid/Fat Beats
Year: 2004
Cat#: OME-2015

"The Pink Cookies" record continues the same themes of volumes three and four, offering more instrumentals from a variety of J Zone recordings. Record comes in a plain white sleeve.

Artist: J Zone
Title: "A Job Ain't Nuthin But Work" Instrumentals
Format: LP
Producer: J Zone
Label: Old Maid/Fat Beats
Year: 2004
Cat#: OME-2016

Volume seven with the tan label offers instrumentals from Zone's "A Job Ain't Nuthin But Work" album. Self explanatory, right? Record comes in a plain white sleeve.

Artist: J Zone
Title: "Sick Of Being Rich" Instrumentals
Format: 2LP
Producer: J Zone
Label: Old Maid/Fat Beats
Year: 2003
Cat#: OME-2013-A

This was J Zone's last instrumental LP. Here you'll find all the quirky instrumentals to his "Sick Of Being Rich" LP across two discs. Record comes in a generic black sleeve with a sticker across the top.

Artist: Kero One
Title: "Windmills Of The Soul" Instrumentals
Format: 2LP
Producers: Kero One, King Most
Label: Plug Label
Year: 2007
Cat#: P00005i

On the production side, "Windmills Of The Soul" represents some of Kero's best work steeped in Jazz rhythms. Look no further if you're into Jazzy Hip Hop. "Windmills" is loaded with electric keys, horns, piano, bass, brushed snares and funky drum programming. Record comes in a picture sleeve.

Artist: Kev Brown
Title: "I Do What I Do" Instrumentals
Format: 2LP
Producer: Kev Brown
Label: Up Above
Year: 2006
Cat#: UPA3118-1

Kev Brown is one of the main reasons why I had to retire my MPC. He represented the type of sound I was looking for when it came to making beats, and he made it look so easy and sound so good. This release on the Up Above label was a limited edition LP pressed on brown marbled vinyl. You'll find all the incredible production from his "I Do What I Do" album here. Album also comes in a picture sleeve.

Artist: Kev Brown
Title: "Songs Without Words Vol. 1" Instrumentals
Format: LP
Producer: Kev Brown
Label: Redef/Low Budget
Year: 2013
Cat#: LB007

Here's one of the latest releases from Kev Brown on Redef Records. It's a collection of beats produced by Kev Brown you may have heard on other recordings. Some previously unreleased and unheard material is also featured on here. Album comes in a picture sleeve.

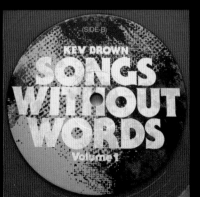

Artist: Kev Brown
Title: "Songs Without Words Vol. 1" (Limited Orange) Instrumentals
Format: LP
Producer: Kev Brown
Label: Redef/Low Budget
Year: 2013
Cat#: LB007

Same description as the first record, but this one is the limited edition pressing on orange vinyl. I believe only 500 copies of this version were made. Album also comes in a picture sleeve.

Artist: Kev Brown
Title: "Songs Without Words Vol. 2, Green Instrumentals"
Format: LP
Producer: Kev Brown
Label: Redef/Low Budget
Year: 2013
Cat#: LB008

Redef and Low Budget records released an album a few years ago by Kaimbr and Kev Brown called "The Alexander Green Project." The concept behind the production on that particular album was to use nothing but Al Green samples. These are the brilliantly constructed instrumentals from that original vocal album pressed on green/black gamma ray swirl vinyl. Album comes in a picture sleeve designed by Joe Buck.

Artist: King Britt
Title: "Adventures In Lo-Fi" Instrumentals
Format: 2LP
Producer: King Britt
Label: BBE
Year: 2003
Cat#: LC 07306

There was a time when BBE was one of the best labels for quality Hop Hop releases. They would sometimes release these instrumental versions to albums, like the Jazzy Jeff album you saw earlier. This time we have the instrumental version to King Britt's release, "Adventures In Lo-Fi." You'll find a lot of mid to high tempo beats on here, all funky. Record comes in a black sleeve with a sticker across the top.

Artist: King Solomon
Title: "Solstice" Instrumentals
Format: LP
Producer: King Solomon
Label: Illmindmuzik
Year: 2003
Cat#: B376352-01

I'm really not too familiar with King Solomon's music as an MC. I basically found this record by accident, but upon listening to it, I found some really nice beats on here. It sounds like King Solomon may draw some of his production influences from Madlib or Ta'Raach. Album comes in a plain black sleeve.

Artist: Kool Keith
Title: "Sex Style" Instrumentals
Format: 2LP
Producer: Kut Masta Kurt
Label: Funky Ass
Year: 1999
Cat#: KTR013-1

At first Kool Keith released a limited edition EP under the name Big Willie Smith on Funky Ass Records, which is one of his most expensive and sought after records. Some of the same songs and Big Willie themes from that EP ended up on "Sex Style." This album is straight amateur POV, Lone Ranger mask wearin', sketchy Vegas Motel 6 fetish-creeper porno-style Hip Hop. Record comes in a black sleeve with a sticker in the top left hand corner.

Artist: Kool Keith
Title: "Matthew" Instrumentals
Format: 2LP
Producer: Kut Masta Kurt
Label: Funky Ass
Year: 2000
Cat#: THR-3015-1

As a producer, Kut Masta Kurt seems like he can do just about anything with a sampler. Create any sound or any style for the envelope-pushing albums by Kool Keith. That takes some skill. You'll find more oddball greatness on this LP. Record comes in a black sleeve with a sticker in the top left hand corner.

Artist: Kool Keith
Title: "Diesel Truckers" Instrumentals
Format: 2LP
Producer: Kut Masta Kurt
Label: Funky Ass
Year: 2004
Cat#: DMT88009-1

I can just imagine Kool Keith and Kut Masta Kurt writing down their goofiest ideas on pieces of paper, putting them into a hat, and drawing pieces of paper to choose the theme for the new album. "Okay, it's Diesel Truckers!" I mean, who else comes up with this shit? You'll find some really nice production on this record. Album comes in a generic black sleeve with a sticker down the right hand side.

Artist: K-Otix
Title: "Spontaneity" Instrumentals
Format: LP
Producer: The Are
Label: K-Otix Entertainment
Year: 2006
Cat#: AR 14145 Hot Waxx

I spoke to The Are years ago via Myspace (when people were still using that) about this particular record from Japan. He told me he pressed a small number of these just for the Japanese market. You couldn't get these here in the States. The album gives you the instrumentals from the "Spontaneity" album The Are produced for K-Otix. Record comes in a generic black sleeve.

Artist: Lacks
Title: "Re:Lacks Vol 1." Instrumentals
Format: LP
Producer: Ta'Raach
Label: Shaman Works
Year: 2003
Cat#: SXV005

Ta'Raach is one of those producers who have a sound much like Madlib, Kankick or J Dilla. His beats are bass-heavy and sample-rich behind crisp snares and punchy kicks, and usually trot along at a leisurely pace. Record comes in a picture sleeve.

Artist: Lewis Parker
Title: "The Big Game" Instrumentals
Format: LP
Producer: Lewis Parker
Label: King Underground/World Of Dusty Vinyl
Year: 2012
Cat#: KU/WODV-005

This record really has some amazing production by Lewis Parker. The beats sound like complete songs played by musicians scoring a blacksploitation spy thriller. It's brilliant. It's definitely one of the best releases of 2012. Album comes in a picture sleeve resembling a brown record mailer.

Artist: Little Brother
Title: "The Listening" Instrumentals
Format: 2LP
Producer: 9th Wonder
Label: ABB
Year: 2002
Cat#: ABB1050-1INT

ABB has had a solid run of Hip Hop releases since they got their start back in 1997. They introduced the world to Defari, Dilated Peoples, The Sound Providers, and Little Brother. Little Brother's debut album "The Listening" was an instant classic. Record comes in a white sleeve with a sticker across the top.

Artist: Lone Catalysts
Title: "Hip Hop" Instrumentals
Format: 2LP
Producer: J Rawls
Label: B.U.K.A.
Year: 2001
Cat#: LCHH01-3

Here's one of my favorite records with production from J Rawls: the instrumental version to the Lone Catalysts debut album released under Grooveattack in Germany. It's not particularly rare, but it's one of those records that's solid from beginning to end, thanks to J Rawls' filtered beats. Record comes in a generic white sleeve.

Artist: The Lootpack
Title: "Soundpieces: Da Antidote" Instrumentals
Format: 2LP
Producer: Madlib
Year: 1999
Cat#: STH2020

The groundbreaking debut LP by the Lootpack features early production by the now well-known producer Madlib. The beats are extra SP1200 dirty on this one. Record comes in a generic black sleeve and has been re-pressed a number of times.

Artist: Lord Finesse
Title: "The Awakening" Instrumentals
Format: LP
Producer: Lord Finesse
Label: Penalty
Year: 1996
Cat#: PREP 3039

As an MC, Lord Finesse is known for his distinct voice and impressive punch lines, but he's also known for crafting some of the illest beats on the SP1200. Which brings us to his 1996 release on Penalty. The EP, which featured guest appearances by Roy Ayers, O.C., KRS-One, Grand Puba and Sadat X, came with a vocal disc and a limited edition bonus instrumental LP. Original album comes in a picture sleeve, while promo versions come in a generic black sleeve with a sticker at the top.

Artist: Lord Finesse
Title: "Instrumentals"
Format: LP
Producer: Lord Finesse
Label: Soundtable
Year: 2006
Cat#: SPED-777

Released in Japan under Soundtable, this record offers a selection of unreleased beats by Lord Finesse. Some of the recordings you'll find on here appeared in songs , but some were intended for songs that remain unreleased. Beats for, or used by Big L, Showbiz & AG, Grand Puba, Xperado, Ill Biskits, and freestyle sessions by Finesse on the Stretch & Bobbito show. Album comes in a generic black sleeve.

Artist: Lord Finesse & DJ Mike Smooth
Title: "Funky Technician" Instrumentals Test Pressing
Format: 2LP
Producers: DJ Premier, Diamond D, Showbiz, DJ Mike Smooth
Label: Slice Of Spice/Underboss
Year: 2012
Cat# SSR-007

One of my prized records from the stash— a signed and numbered copy of the test for the "Funky Technician" instrumentals. Record is an 180g pressing and comes inside a white gatefold sleeve with a sticker pasted in the middle of the front cover. Black labels stamped with Slice Of Spice Records and Lord Finesse Logos.

Artist: Lord Finesse & DJ Mike Smooth
Title: "Funky Technician" Instrumentals (Limited Gold Version)
Format: 2LP
Producers: DJ Premier, Diamond D, Showbiz, DJ Mike Smooth
Label: Slice Of Spice/Underboss
Year: 2012
Cat# SSR-007

22 years after the original Lord Finesse and DJ Mike Smooth album was released on Wild Pitch we finally see the instrumentals in their full glory. Pressed on limited edition 180g gold vinyl, the album also comes in a numbered gatefold sleeve with cover art and design by the great Joe Buck and Mr. Krum. Classic beats right here.

Artist: Lord Finesse & DJ Mike Smooth
Title: "Funky Technician" Instrumentals
Format: 2LP
Producers: DJ Premier, Diamond D, Showbiz, DJ Mike Smooth
Label: Slice Of Spice/Underboss
Year: 2012
Cat# SSR-007

I like to include all the available variations of an album if I can, especially for one this nice. Here's what the normal release for this LP pressed on standard black vinyl looks like. Same gatefold cover and artwork as the limited gold pressing and also pressed on 180g vinyl.

Artist: Lord Finesse
Title: "The Prequel" Instrumentals Test Press
Format: LP
Producers: Lord Finesse, Large Professor, Showbiz
Label: Slice Of Spice/Underboss
Year: 2013
Cat#: SSR-026

A recent release on the Slice Of Spice label archives, with instrumentals recorded 22 years ago by Lord Finesse during the "Return Of The Funkman" era and pressed on 180g vinyl. You'll find some incredible beats on here, like "Isn't He Something (Showbiz remix)," "Funky On The Fast Tip" and "Isn't He Something (Large Pro remix)." Vocal versions can be found on the "Funky Man: The Prequel" LP. Record comes in a black sleeve with stamped labels and a sticker pasted in the middle of the cover. Limited to 10 copies.

Artist: Lord Finesse
Title: "The Prequel" Instrumentals Limited Edition (White Vinyl)
Format: LP
Producers: Lord Finesse, Large Professor, Showbiz
Label: Slice Of Spice/Underboss
Year: 2013
Cat#: SSR-026

Same description as the Prequel test pressing, only this time these instrumentals are pressed on a limited edition number of only 200 copies made on white 180g vinyl. Album comes in a picture sleeve with silver foil and is numbered #1/200.

Artist: Lord Finesse
Title: "The Prequel" Instrumentals
Format: LP
Producers: Lord Finesse, Large Professor, Showbiz
Label: Slice Of Spice/Underboss
Year: 2013
Cat#: SSR-026

Here's what the commercial release for "The Prequel" instrumentals looks like. Pressed on standard black 180g vinyl, only 300 copies made. Album comes in a picture sleeve.

Artist: Various
Title: "Lyricist Lounge Vol. 2" Instrumentals
Format: 2LP
Producers: Roddy Rod, DJ Premier, Hi Tek Jay Dee, Alchemist, DJ Mighty Mi
Label: Rawkus
Year: 2000
Cat#: RWK-1191

Volume two was the only Lyricist Lounge album that also had an instrumental version release. It's one of the more common instrumental LPs Rawkus made, and one of the cheapest at market price. I still come across this one quite often for less than ten bucks. Album comes in a black sleeve with the typical Rawkus sticker in the top left hand corner.

Artist: Madvillain
Title: "Madvillainy" Instrumentals
Format: 2LP
Producer: Madlib
Label: Stones Throw
Year: 2004
Cat#: STH2099

The Madvillainy album has really gained a large cult following with fans of MF Doom and Madlib. The collaboration was genius, so this album never really went out of print. The first pressing had blue text on the label, while all the other re-presses had white text on the label. The most recent pressing also had a full picture sleeve. Album comes in a generic black sleeve.

Artist: Marco Polo
Title: "Rare Instrumentals No.1"
Format: LP
Producer: Marco Polo
Label: Street Symphony
Year: 2013
Cat#: SSR003

Street Symphony Records teamed up with Marco Polo for this limited edition release featuring unreleased instrumental tracks. You'll find beats used for songs recorded by such artist as Talib Kweli, Neek The Exotic, Grand Daddy I.U., Sadat X, AG, JuJu and Vinnie Paz, among others. Record comes in a picture sleeve. Import.

Artist: Mark B & Blade
Title: "The Unknown" Instrumentals
Format: 2LP
Producer: Mark B
Label: Wordplay
Year: 2000
Cat#: WORDLP012

Unfortunately, imports like these from artists like Mark B & Blade were not something you could just go out and buy here in the States. You always had to track these down online, usually for a crazy exchange rate with shipping costs added on top. Local used record stores really come to the rescue when it comes to obscure releases like these. I found this instrumental version of "The Unknown" locally for less than ten bucks. You'll find a solid selection of funky beats on this one. Record comes in a plain black sleeve with a sticker in the top left hand corner.

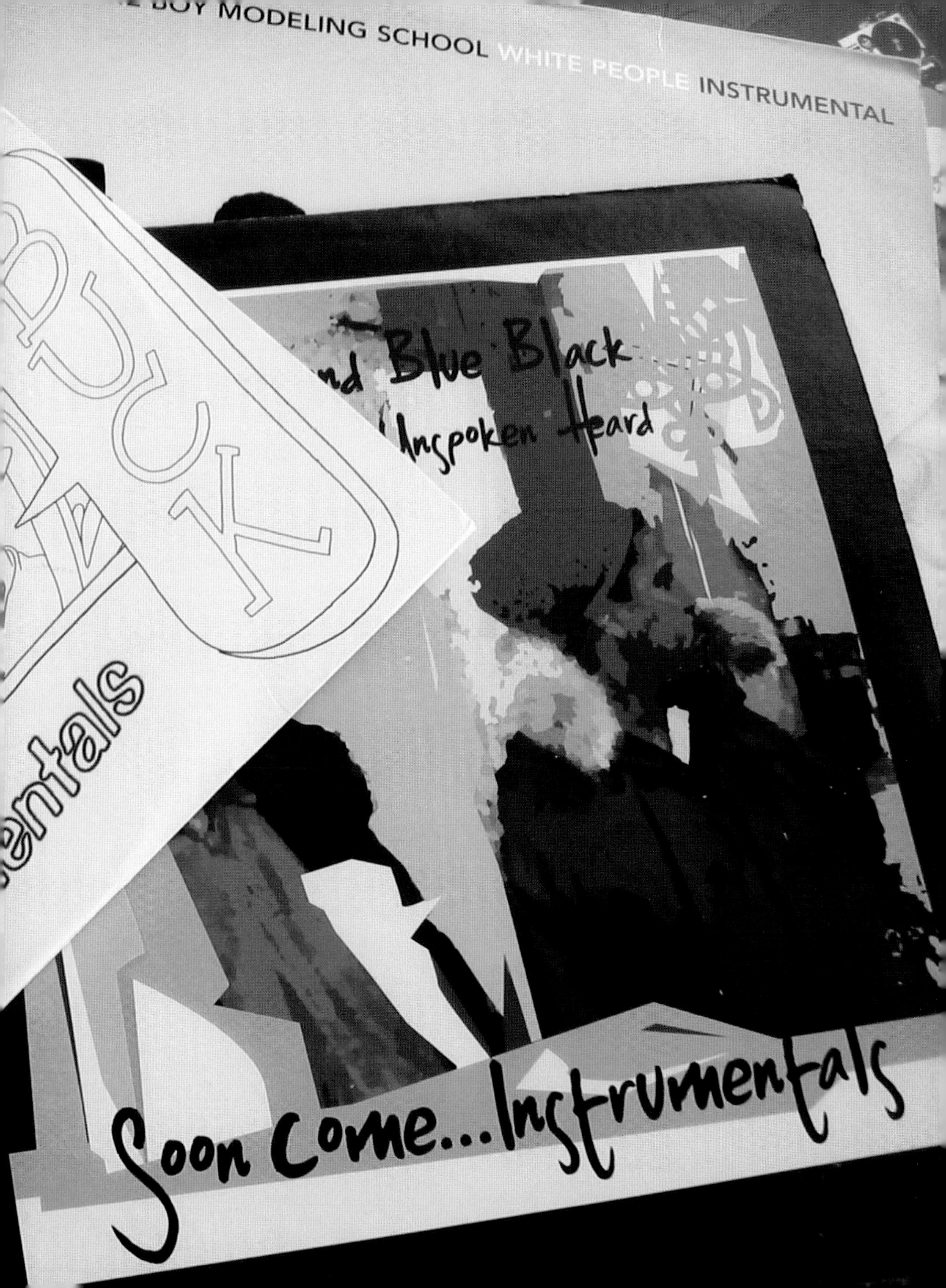

nd Blue Black

Unspoken Heard

entals

Soon Come...Instrumentals

Artist: Masta Ace
Title: "Brooklyn Dubs" Instrumentals
Format: LP
Producers: Ase One, Blues Brothers
Label: South Paw
Year: 1996
Cat#: S-3149

Back when this record was first released in '96, I just figured it was just a breakbeat/party breaks record called "Brooklyn Dubs." Those were popular at the time. It wasn't until many years later that someone told me this had Masta Ace instrumentals on it. The EP offers a selection of beats from Masta Ace's "Sittin On Chrome" LP you couldn't find anywhere else. Album comes in a generic white sleeve.

Artist: The Masters Of Illusion
Title: "Masters Of Illusions" Instrumentals
Format: 2LP
Producer: Kut Masta Kurt
Label: Threshold
Year: 2003
Cat#: THR1973A

This is one of the best Kool Keith affiliated albums featuring Motion Man in my opinion. Dope beats, drama, sex and comedy are all a wrapped up in this well crafted concept record. Check out "Souped Up," "We All Over" and my personal favorite, "Let Me Talk To You." Album comes in an illustrated picture sleeve.

Artist: Masterminds
Title: "The Underground Railroad" Instrumentals
Format: 2LP
Producer: Masterminds
Label: Ground Control/Nu Gruv Alliance
Year: 2000
Cat#: GCR 7030

I didn't get into the vocal version of this album too much, other than the singles. So I'm happy Nu Gruv released it as an instrumental. This is one of their more uncommon instrumental releases and features some great production by the Masterminds. Record comes in a generic black sleeve.

Artist: McEnroe
Title: "Druidry" Instrumentals
Format: LP
Producer: McEnroe
Label: Peanuts & Corn
Year: 2002
Cat#: PC018

I found this first record in the dollar bin one day, took a chance on it, and liked it. Later, I discovered more Peanuts & Corn releases, which were kind of hard to find in the first place. Peanuts & Corn records are obscure Canadian releases in general, but worth tracking down. McEnroe's beats here are mellow and a little bit on the dark side. Record comes in a generic white sleeve.

Artist: McEnroe
Title: "All Beef, No Chicken" Instrumentals
Format: LP
Producers: McEnroe, Hunnicutt
Label: Peanuts & Corn
Year: 2003
Cat#: P&Ci02

I used to have the vocal version to this LP with a pack of wieners on the front cover. This is another obscure release from P&C with real solid production. McEnroe might just be one of the best producers you never heard of. Prolific, too. There are a number of releases on this label produced by McEnroe worth checking out. One of the standout cuts on here is "Brains & Brawn." Record comes in a plain white sleeve.

Artist: MED
Title: "Push Comes To Shove" Instrumentals
Format: 2LP
Producers: Madlib, J Dilla, Oh No, Just Blaze
Label: Stones Throw
Year: 2005
Cat#: STH2114

MED's albums always had really dope production. I was never a huge fan of his as a MC but the instrumentals work out just fine. Album comes in a generic black sleeve.

Artist: M.E.D
Title: "Classic" Instrumentals
Format: LP
Producers: Madlib, Georgia Anne Muldrow, The Alchemist
Label: Stones Throw
Year: 2011
Cat#: STH2275

Unfortunately, the only way to get a copy of this album was if to pay thirty bucks for the limited edition 3LP deluxe version. The deluxe version came with the normal 2LP album release and this bonus instrumental disc. Also, if you listen to the album and compare tracks on the instrumental disc, you'll notice some beats missing, including one of my favorite beats with a nice guitar loop. Record comes in a black sleeve with track title listings.

Artist: MF Doom
Title: "Special Herbs Vol 1" Instrumentals
Format: LP
Producers: MF Doom, DJ Spinna
Label: Female Fun/Metal Fingers
Year: 2000
Cat#: FF001

This was the first ever Special Herbs releases on the Female Fun label. Little did I know that about a thousand other Special Herbs releases would soon follow, all featuring beats from MF Doom recordings. The first pressing in the series came with a picture sleeve and had comic book style artwork on the cover. I like how the label design on this pressing is comic book inspired as well.

Artist: MF Doom
Title: "Special Herbs Vol. 1 & 2" Instrumentals
Format: 2LP
Producers: MF Doom, DJ Spinna
Label: High Times
Year: 2003
Cat#: HTR-105

This is the second pressing of "Special Herbs Vol. 1" released by High Times Records. This version came as a 2LP pressing inside a gatefold cover. Same artwork as the original pressing, only this time the disc is labeled "Special Herbs Vol. 2."

Artist: MF Doom
Tilte: "Special Herbs Vol. 4, 5, & 6" Instrumentals
Format: 2LP
Producer: MF Doom
Label: Shawman Work
Year: 2003
Cat#: SW004-1

There are just too many Special Herbs albums to keep up with, so I'll just mention the first three. Here's the third release in the Special Herbs series, which totally skipped over Vol.3 and went straight to 4. This release also had comic book inspired artwork for the cover design, which caused an uproar over at Marvel Comics because of the unauthorized use of their Dr. Doom character. The album was pulled from store shelves and later re-pressed with a totally different cover.

Artist: DJ Mitsu The Beats
Title: "A Word To The Wise" Instrumentals
Format: 2LP
Producer: DJ Mitsu
Label: Planetgroove
Year: 2009
Cat#: PGLP-P1006

The original vocal version of this record was a 3LP pressing that featured various instrumental tracks and songs with guest appearances by Grap Luva, LMNO, and Maspyke, among many other artists. You'll find all the instrumentals to the original vocal tracks from the "Word To The Wise" LP here. Record comes in a generic black sleeve. Japanese import.

Artist: DJ Mitsu The Beats
Title: "Universal Force" Instrumentals
Format: 2LP
Producer: DJ Mitsu
Label: Jazzy Sport
Year: 2010
Cat#: JSV-093/094

The original vocal version of this album was in Japanese, so I would definitely need a translator just to know what I was listening to. But you can't go wrong with the music. DJ Mitsu's beats are universal (no pun intended). Album is a limited edition pressing of 300 copies and comes in a black sleeve with a green sticker across the top.

Artist: Mos Def
Title: "Black On Both Sides" Instrumentals
Format: 2LP
Producers: DJ Premier, 88 Keys, Ayatollah, Ali Shaheed Muhamed
Label: Rawkus
Year: 1999
Cat#: RWK 1175

Arguably the most enjoyable and the most solid album ever recorded from Mos Def. You'll find songs like "Universal Magnetic," "If You Can Huh," "Mathmatics," "Umi Says" and "Mrs. Fat Booty" on here. Record comes in a generic black sleeve with a sticker in the top left hand corner.

Artist: Motion Man
Title: "Clearing The Field" Instrumentals
Format: 2LP
Producer: Kut Masta Kurt
Label: Threshold
Year: 2002
Cat#: THR-5103

One of my favorite releases from Kut Masta Kurt featuring Motion Man, mostly for the humor and beats. Original LP featured guest appearances by E40, Biz Markie, Planet Asia and Kool Keith. Instrumental version comes in a picture sleeve designed like an action figure package with a real action figure of Kut Masta Kurt on the front cover. I wonder where they had those made?

Artist: The Mountain Brothers
Title: "Self Vol. 1" Instrumentals
Format: LP
Producer: Chops
Label: Mountain Brothers
Year: 1998
Cat#: MBINST1

Chops "The Magnificent Butcher" had a signature sound and production style. I'm almost 100% positive that he composed everything on an ASR10 keyboard like a skilled musician, without the use of sampled loops. This particular record is a private pressing on the Mountain Brothers label with instrumentals from the Mountain Brothers debut album, "Self Volume 1." You might remember songs like "Galaxies," "Paperchase" and "Optometry" from the group. Album comes in a generic black sleeve.

Artist: DJ Muro
Title: "Japanese Gangster" Instrumentals
Format: LP
Producer: Muro
Label: Prime Cuts
Year: 2008
Cat#: JGEP001

DJ Muro remixed and released a version of Jay Z's "American Gangster" album on CD. This record features a small selection of the beats found on that remix album. Record comes in a white sleeve with a blue sticker at the top.

Artist: Mykill Miers
Title: "It's Been A Long Time" Instrumentals
Format: 2LP
Producers: Cheapshot, M Boogie, Amed, Diverse, Voodu
Label: Blackberry/Ill Boogie
Year: 2000
Cat#: ILL72021

I found a copy of this record with the same label pressed on both discs. An obvious manufacturing mistake that I've never seen before, which I'm taking offers on for its ultra-rarity factor if anyone is interested— no, I'm playin'. But seriously, this is a dope record with top notch production from the small lineup of producers you see featured here. Album comes in a picture sleeve with the words "The Instrumentals" printed in red at the bottom of the cover.

Artist: Nathaniel Merriweather
Title: "Lovage, Music To Make Love To Your Old Lady By" Instrumentals
Format: 2LP
Producer: Dan the Automator
Label: 75ARK
Year: 2001
Cat#: AK5053

This record should come standard with a bottle of Sex Panther cologne. It's what I would describe as a brilliantly crafted comedy album exploring love and lust, with lounge inspired beats and intentional cheesiness. A classic. Album comes in a picture sleeve with cover art mocking Serge Gainsbourg's "No. 2" album.

Artist: The Nextmen
Title: "Amongst The Madness"
Format: 2LP
Producer: The Nextmen
Label: Scenario
Year: 2000
Cat#: SCLPINS004

One of the most overlooked and underappreciated albums by the UK production team The Nextmen. Original album features vocals by Grap Luva, Ty, Asheru, Soulson and Ken Boogaloo. Record comes in a plain white sleeve with a red sticker in the top right hand corner.

Artist: 9th Wonder
Title: "God's Stepson" Instrumentals
Format: 2LP
Producer: 9th Wonder
Label: HipHopSite
Year: 2004
Cat#: HHS-005

Instrumental version of a remix project produced by 9th Wonder for HipHopSite.com, using the full vocal content of the "God Son" LP by Nas. Record comes in a generic black sleeve.

Artist: Non Phixion
Title: "The Future Is Now" Instrumentals
Format: 2LP
Producers: Large Professor, Pete Rock, DJ Premier, JuJu
Label: Uncle Howie
Year: 2003
Cat#: UHR013

There's so many good beats to choose from on this particular album. I mean, just look at the high-powered list of producers who worked on this record. Album comes in an Uncle Howie sleeve with a sticker in the top right hand corner.

Artist: Oh No
Title: "The Disrupt" Instrumentals
Format: 2LP
Producers: Oh No, J Dilla, Kankick
Label: Stones Throw
Year: 2005
Cat#: STH2104

I forgot how unbelievably dope this record actually is. One of my favorite cuts on here, and one of Madlib's grooviest beats, is called "Every Section." Another highlight for me is the Kankick produced track, "Take Another." Album comes in a generic black sleeve.

Artist: Oh No
Title: "Exodus Into Unheard Rhythms" Instrumentals
Fornat: 2LP
Producer: Oh No
Label: Stones Throw
Year: 2006
Cat#: STH2146

Oh No's "Exodus Into Unheard Rhythms" is an album constructed using only Galt MacDermot samples. He even lifted samples from the album "Ghetto Suite," an album composed of poems written by inner city children. The result is pretty amazing. Instrumental album comes in a generic white sleeve.

Artist: Peanut Butter Wolf
Title: "My Vinyl Weights A Ton" Instrumentals
Format: 2LP
Producer: Peanut Butter Wolf
Label: Stones Throw
Year: 1998
Cat#: STH2071i

This is probably the last record PB Wolf ever made before he retired as a producer to focus on his record label ventures. The original LP for "My Vinyl Weighs A Ton" was a special triple disc album featuring Rasco, Lootpack, Quasimoto, DJ Babu, Charizma, Q-Bert, Beat Junkies... the list goes on and on. The original album was also later re-pressed as a double LP, which brings us to the limited edition instrumental pressing. I believe most of the beats from the album are found on this LP. Record comes in a generic black sleeve.

Artist: People Under The Stairs
Title: "Question In The Form Of An Answer" Instrumentals
Format: LP
Producers: Thes One, Double K
Label: OM
Year: 2000
Cat#: OM-044LP

Unfortunately, PUTS has never released a full length instrumental album for any of their releases, which is a shame because their production is amazing. The three instrumental records that have been pressed are more like EPs than actual full length albums. For example, this first pressing featured a small selection of beats from "Questions In The Form Of An Answer." You'll find beats for songs like "San Francisco Knights," "Live At The Fishbucket Pt. 1" and "Blowin Wax," just to name a few. Record comes in a picture sleeve with labels made to look like CTI Records.

Artist: People Under The Stairs
Title: "Stepfather Pt. 1" Instrumentals
Format: LP
Producers: Double K, Thes One
Label: Tres
Year: 2007
Cat#: TR396-019

Part one features a small selection of beats from the first half of the "Stepfather" LP. You'll find instrumentals for "Step In," "Pumpin," "Flex Off," "Days Like This," "Jamboree Pt. 1" and "Jamboree Pt. 2." Album comes in an orange picture sleeve.

Artist: People Under The Stairs
Title: "Stepfather Pt. 2" Instrumentals
Format: LP
Producers: Thes One, Double K, Kat Ouano
Label: Tres
Year: 2007
Cat#: TR396-025

Part two is just like part one. It has a small selection of beats from the second half of the "Stepfather" LP. "Eat Street," "Crown Ones," "LA9X," "The Brown Out," "You" and "On And On (Alternate)." Both editions are still pretty easy to track down for less than ten bucks, on average. Prices should be higher in my opinion, but I'm not really all that surprised either.

Artist: Percee P
Title: "Perseverance" Instrumentals
Format: LP
Producer: Madlib
Label: Stones Throw
Year: 2008
Cat#: STH2178

I met the legendary Percee P at one of the Bay Area editions of the Beat Swap Meet recently and the guy was incredibly cool and humble. Now when I look back at that day, I wish I had a copy of this record with me for him to sign. You'll find most of the instrumentals from his debut album here, produced entirely by Madlib. Record comes in a generic black sleeve.

Artist: Pete Rock
Title: "Soul Survivor II" Instrumentals
Format: 2LP
Producer: Pete Rock
Label: BBE/Rapster
Year: 2004
Cat#: PR0032

I recently found a second sealed copy of this record at a local shop priced for less than ten bucks, which shows you a little bit about how underrated this album actually is. The first "Soul Survivor" is a certified classic but this one just didn't get as much shine. The beats are dope, though. Album comes in a black sleeve with a sticker across the top.

Artist: Pete Rock
Title: "NY's Finest" Instrumentals
Format: 2LP
Producer: Pete Rock
Label: Nature Sounds
Year: 2008
Cat#: NSD137

I just had to buy two copies of this one when it was released. Pressed as a limited edition instrumental LP, you'll find all the beats from "NY's Finest," with two bonus beats unavailable on the original album. Record comes in a picture sleeve reminiscent of James Brown's "Hell" album.

Artist: The Pharcyde
Title: "Bizarre Ride II The Pharcyde" Instrumentals
Format: LP
Producers: J Swift, LA Jay, Tre Hardson
Label: Delicious Vinyl
Year: 2004
Cat#: DV77221

I found a copy of the original show vinyl for this record a few years after Delicious Vinyl pressed these in 2004 in our promo/show vinyl section. The beats are a little different compared to the original test pressing, and there's more straightforward instrumental tracks here. If you listen to both records and compare the two, you'll find choruses, vocal dubs and other atmospheric elements missing from this new version. Also, the instrumental for "Pack The Pipe" is missing on the commercial release. Album comes in a blue picture sleeve.

Artist: The Pharcyde
Title: "Labcabincalifornia" Instrumentals
Format: 2LP
Producers: Dismond D, Jay Dee, The Pharcyde
Label: Delicious Vinyl
Year: 2004
Cat#: DV77229-1

I'm pretty sure these instrumentals were originally a show vinyl pressing since groups were still using DJs during live performances in 1996. Or maybe they just sat on 2" reels on some shelf in a closet somewhere, collecting dust, until this release in 2004. You'll find all the instrumentals to the Pharcyde's sophomore release, with early beats by Jay Dee (J Dilla) and Diamond D. Record comes in a picture sleeve.

Artist: Pharoahe Monch
Title: "Internal Affairs" Instrumentals
Format: 2LP
Producers: Diamond D, Pharoahe Monch, Alchemist, DJ Scratch
Label: Rawkus
Year: 1999
Cat#: RWK1174

I see this album more than any other instrumental release on Rawkus Records. It's very common to see sealed copies of the record for ten dollars or less. Maybe Rawkus just pressed too many of these due to the fact that the lead single, "Simon Says," became a huge hit. I mean, you couldn't go anywhere without hearing the words "Get the fuck up! Simon says 'Get the fuck up!'" Clubs, radio, the grocery store... Album comes in a black sleeve with a sticker in the top left hand corner.

Artist: Phife
Title: "Ventilation" Instrumentals
Format: 2LP
Producers: Pete Rock, Hi Tek, Jay Dee
Label: Landspeed/Grooveattack
Year: 2000
Cat#: GAP068

As an instrumental album with really dope production from Jay Dee and Pete Rock, you'd think this one would prove extremely difficult to track down. But it's not — it's a very common record. A definite sleeper. Album comes in a plain white sleeve.

Artist: Platinum Pied Pipers
Title: "Triple P" Instrumentals
Format: 2LP
Producers: Wajeed, Mark De Clive Lowe
Label: Ubiquity
Year: 2006
Cat#: URLP 190

Instrumental album from the triple Ps that carries that Detroit sound J Dilla made so famous. The album also offers two bonus beats that were previously not used on the original vocal LP. Album is fairly common and comes in a generic white sleeve with a sticker across the top.

Artist: Planet Asia
Title: "Planet Asia" Instrumentals
Format: LP
Producer: Fanatik
Label: Heratik
Year: 1998
Cat#: HTK-003

Planet Asia's debut LP had a promising young Bay Area producer on the beats who went by the studio name Fanatik. I hadn't listened to this record in a long time, but recently, while going back to reference it, I realized that two of the beats on this LP were lifted from Fanatik's "Nothin But A Beat Thang" album released on Stones Throw back in '97. Record comes in a glossy white sleeve.

Artist: Porn Theatre Ushers
Title: "Sloppy Seconds" Instrumentals
Format: 2LP
Producer: Mr. Jason
Label: Biscuit Head/Land Speed
Year: 2000
Cat#: BHR- 1003

Random release by an equally random group at the time called Porn Theatre Ushers with dope beats. Producer Mr. Jason is still producing well-crafted rap tunes. Album comes in a picture sleeve with bonus instrumental disc.

Artist: Q-Unique
Title: "Vengeance Is Mine" Instrumentals
Format: 2LP
Producers: Q-Unique, Necro, JuJu, Context, Pase One
Label: Uncle Howie
Year: 2005
Cat#: UHR023

I received a couple of really solid 12" singles from Q-Unique through the record pool I was in during the late '90s. All of those singles had really great production on them, which definitely influenced my purchase of the instrumental LP. Record comes in a red and white Uncle Howie sleeve with a red sticker in the top right hand corner.

Artist: Various
Title: "Quannum Spectrum" Instrumentals
Format: 2LP
Producers: DJ Shadow, Chief Xcel, Lyrics Born
Label: Mo Wax/Quannum Projects
Year: 1999
Cat#: MWR110LPS

Instrumental version to a solid compilation album featuring Quannum Project crew members Blackalicious, DJ Shadow, Lyrics Born, and Latyrix, among many other guest appearances. Album comes in a white picture sleeve.

Artist: Quasimoto
Title: "The Unseen" Instrumentals
Format: 2LP
Producer: Madlib
Label: Stones Throw
Year: 2000
Cat#: STH206-1

I didn't really know what to think when I first heard a Quasimoto record. The vocals sounded like Madlib hooked a helium tank to the vocal booth. I think the first Quasi single I ever recieved as a promo was "Come On Feet," which was a weird record, but also way ahead of its time. The weed stash must've been incredible that day. The is album offers some of Madlib's best, quirkiest and most creative work on the production side. Album comes in a plain black sleeve. Represses have darker yellow labels compared to the original pressing, which has a much brighter yellow label.

Artist: Quasimoto
Title: "The Further Adventures Of Lord Quas" Instrumentals
Format: 2LP
Producer: Madlib
Label: Stones Throw
Year: 2005
Cat#: STH2116

Here are the full length instrumentals to the second album by Quasimoto, Madlib's helium-voiced alter ego. More fat beats and quirky samples are featured on this one as well. Instrumental LP originally came in a plain black sleeve, but Stones Throw is now re-releasing them with a full picture sleeve for collectors.

Artist: Rasco
Title: "Time Waits For No Man" Instrumentals
Format: 2LP
Producers: Paul Nice, Protest, Kut Masta Kurt, Fanatik, Joey Chavez, Evidence, Peanut Butter Wolf, The 45 King
Label: Stones Throw
Year: 1998
Cat#: STH201ai

Rasco's debut album released by Stones Throw shockingly scored a commercial radio hit with the lead single "The Unassisted," produced by Fanatik. The instrumental version was finally released much later with somewhat ambiguous labels, missing the track listings and the Stones Throw logo. The record basically looks like a bootleg. An added bonus on this one is the instrumental track for the 45 King remix for "Run The Line." This is the only place to find that instrumental on vinyl. Album comes in a generic black sleeve.

Artist: Rasco
Title: "The Birth" Instrumentals
Format: 2EP
Producers: Captain Kill A Mothafucka, His-Panik
Label: Copasetik
Year: 1999
Cat#: COPA011

Rasco's second effort on Copasetik has him teaming up with His-Panik from the Molemen for the majority of the record's production, which is a good fit for Rasco's voice. The second disc has all the instrumentals. Record comes in a picture sleeve with a developing fetus on the front cover. This is the most common Rasco album you can find.

Artist: Rasco
Title: "Hostile Environment" Instrumentals
Format: 2LP
Producers: Protest, Roddy Rod, J Rawls, Memo, His-Panik
Label: Copasetik
Year: 2001
Cat#: COPA 025

This is probably the most sacred of all the Rasco instrumental LP releases. I don't remember the last time I saw another copy anywhere. This was also the last release from Rasco on the Copasetik label, rumored to be due to the woes he had with the label and its founder. Record comes in a generic black sleeve.

Artist: Rasco
Title: "Escape From Alcatraz" Instrumentals
Format: 2LP
Poducers: Brisk One, Jake One, Kleph Dollaz, Champ, Omen, Da Beatminerz, Ambush
Label: Pockets Linted
Year: 2003
Cat#: PLE-7021

I initially passed on this album when it was first released and ever since I've had a hard time tracking one down. I finally found a signed NOS copy at a local spot. Of course, now that I have a copy I see this album everywhere. Funny how that happens. Record comes in a picture sleeve. Highlights on this one are beats from Jake One and the Beatminerz.

Artist: DJ Revolution
Title: "In 12's We Trust" Instrumentals
Format: 2LP
Producers: DJ Revolution, Evidence, Joey Chavez
Label: Milenia/Ground Control
Year: 2000
Cat#: GCR7046

I never really got into many Hip Hop albums by scratch DJs or radio personalities. I thought most of those albums were pretty lame — I wasn't trying to listen to 20 minute scratch sessions using "f-f-f-f-fresssh." But there are a few really dope ones out there, like this one from the Wake Up Show's resident DJ. The album was also backed by some really nice beats from Evidence and Joey Chsvez. Sometimes I'd open my radio show with "Take Over" way back when. Record comes in a plain black sleeve.

Artist: RJD2
Title: "Magnificent City" Instrumentals
Format: 2LP
Producer: RJD2
Label: Decon
Year: 2006
Cat#: DCN 38-DLP

Aceyalone released an album produced entirely by RJD2 called "Magnificent City." The instrumental version soon followed, featuring the standalone production genius of producer RJD2. RJD2 won an award for a song called "A Beautiful Mine" on this record, which is used in the opening sequence of the popular and critically acclaimed AMC television series Mad Men. Instrumental LP comes in a picture sleeve.

Artist: Roc Marciano
Title: "Marcberg Beats" Instrumentals
Format: LP
Producer: Roc Marciano
Label: Fatbeats
Year: 2013
Cat#: FB5161

You'll notice the labels on these have "2012" printed at the bottom, but delays pushed this record back to an official release of mid-May 2013. Here you'll find almost all of the beats featured on Roc Marciano's acclaimed debut album. Record also comes in a nice die cut sleeve with the title "Marcberg" cut out of the middle of the front cover.

LOW LIFE'S MAIN CO

'FOOD' INSTRUM

Artist: Screwball
Title: "Y2K" Instrumentals
Format: LP
Producers: DJ Premier, Pete Rock, Vic, Godfather Don, Mike Heron
Label: Hydra
Year: Unknown
Cat#: HYD-731

Tommy Boy records released the original vocal version for this LP, so I'm a little confused as to why the instrumental would be released on Hydra. At any rate, most of the instrumentals from the "Y2K" album are here. One of my favorite beats on this record is "You Love to Hear the Stories," produced by Pete Rock. Album comes in a generic white sleeve.

Artist: Scienz Of Life
Title: "Project Overground" Instrumentals
Format: 2LP
Producers: Scienz Of Life
Label: Sub Level
Year: 2007
Cat#: SVM23

I don't know much about these guys as a group, but I'm a fan of their music and especially their production. You won't be disappointed by these beats. Album comes in a nice picture sleeve.

Artist: 7L & Esoteric
Title: "Dangerous Connection" Instrumentals
Format: LP
Producers: 7L, Beyonder, Stoupe
Label: Brick
Year: 2002
Cat#: BRK 030

This album carries a small selection of beats from 7L & Esoteric's sophomore LP. Album also comes in a generic white sleeve.

Artist: DJ Serious
Title: "Cold Tea" Instrumentals
Format: LP
Producer: DJ Serious
Label: Audio Research
Year: 2005
Cat#: ARC-002

DJ Serious has had a sprinkling of really solid 12" singles over the years, all featuring really great production by Serious. That was what drove me to pick up this album, mostly for the instrumental disc. Album comes in a picture sleeve with a Chinese dragon on the front cover.

Artist: DJ Shadow
Title: "The Outsider" Instrumentals
Format: 2LP
Producer: DJ Shadow
Label: Reconstruction
Year: 2009
Cat#: DJSH-001

These instrumental LPs for DJ Shadow's "The Outsider" are a private pressing on his Reconstruction label. The albums were pressed and marketed as a limited edition 180g double vinyl release inside a thick card stock picture sleeve. The covers were die cut in the middle, revealing a stamped album title, and were all hand numbered with a permanent marker. Labels and inner sleeves are also stamped. To get one you had to order online exclusively through Shadow's website. Some actually ended up being sold in local shops like Amoeba for a brief moment.

Artist: Skhool Yard
Title: "A New Way Of Thinking" Instrumentals
Format: LP
Producers: Kut Masta Kurt, Joey Chavez, Protest
Label: Threshold
Year: 2002
Cat#: THR-2092C

Solid album featuring Planet Asia and Kut Masta Kurt on production. Album also included the instrumentals on disc two. Standout beats include "Cigar Splittas," "Days of Our Lives," and "Sit Back And Chill." Album comes with a picture sleeve.

Artist: Slum Village
Title: "Fantastic Vol.2" Instrumentals
Format: 3LP
Producers: Jay Dee, Pete Rock, D'Angelo
Label: Ne'Astra
Year: 2011
Cat#: NMG35753

"Fantastic Vol. 2": the legendary album produced by James Yancey that ultimately raised the bar and forever changed the game when it came to the craft of making beats. The "Fantastic" instrumentals have been released for the first time ever on this limited edition 3LP set. Album comes inside a six-sided gatefold pictured sleeve with a large limited edition poster.

Artist: Smut Peddlers
Title: "Porn Again" Instrumentals
Format: 2LP
Producer: DJ Mighty Mi
Label: Rawkus
Year: 2001
Cat#: RWK 1200

The Smut Peddlers were more about promoting shock value rather than actually peddling porn-related smut, as the album title and cover (with Beetlejuice from the Howard Stern Show surrounded by porn stars) suggested. Their rhymes were mostly your typical Hip Hop braggadocio, while DJ Mighty Mi continually brought the heat with his strong production. Instrumental album comes in a generic black sleeve with a sticker in the top left hand corner.

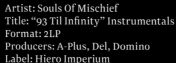

Artist: Souls Of Mischief
Title: "93 Til Infinity" Instrumentals
Format: 2LP
Producers: A-Plus, Del, Domino
Label: Hiero Imperium
Year: 1993
Cat#: HDC LP001A 5-42657

Originally these instrumentals were pressed on a 4LP show vinyl set by Jive Records. Many years later Hiero Imperium released these on a double album set. You'll find all the instrumentals from the Souls Of Mischief's classic debut album on this official release. Record comes in a generic white sleeve.

Artist: Soul Position
Title: "8 Million Stories" Instrumentals
Format: 2LP
Producer: RJD2
Label: Rhymesayers
Year: 2003
Cat#: RS0043-1

RJD2 was a very prolific producer in the early part of the 2000s, releasing some of the most epic and progressive compositions you'll hear on a Hip Hop record. This Soul Position album, produced entirely by RJD2, features some of the complex and amazing beats RJD2 has become famous for. Album comes in a picture sleeve.

Artist: Speech Defect
Title: "Fresh Coast Gettin Rowdy" Instrumentals
Format: LP
Producers: Mr. Linus, Prao-D, Thage
Label: No Cool Music
Year: 2003
Cat#: NCM 006

The first time I came across this one in a local record shop I stashed it in the Joan Baez section so I could come back and buy it later. When I returned the record was unfortunately gone, and it took me a while to track down another one. These guys are a Swedish Hip Hop group with a sound highly influenced by soul and deep funk. I haven't heard beats this funky in a long time. Album comes in a generic white sleeve.

Artist: DJ Spinna
Title: "Compositions" Instrumentals
Format: LP
Producer: DJ Spinna
Label: White
Year: 1996
Cat#: SPIN III

This is the original pressing in the "Compositions" series released by DJ Spinna. The label was made to look like the cover of the composition notebooks we used as kids in school. Here you'll find a selection of beats Spinna produced for a number of obscure remixes he made for artists like MC Eiht and Das Efx, among others. Also included is the coveted instrumental for the "Stakes Is High" remix he produced for De La Soul. This is the only way to get that instrumental. Record comes in a generic white sleeve.

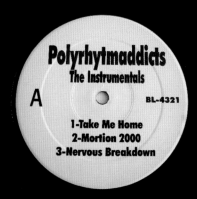

Artist: DJ Spinna
Title: "Rhyme Related" Instrumentals
Format: EP
Producer: DJ Spinna
Label: White
Year: unknown
Cat#: BL-4321

This one is included in the DJ Spinna section because it really is just a DJ Spinna record. It's a white label instrumental release of the Polyrhythmaddicts debut album originally released on Wreck Records. My guess is that this is a private pressing released by DJ Spinna himself, as the vinyl quality is consistent with other Wreck releases at the time. The mastering and overall sound quality on this record is excellent. The group's name and track A2 just happen to be misspelled. Record comes in a generic white sleeve.

Artist: DJ Spinna
Title: "Compositions Vol. 1" Instrumentals
Format: LP
Producer: DJ Spinna
Label: Female Fun/Crosstalk
Year: 2005
Cat#: FF000

Re-press of the original "Compositions" EP from DJ Spinna on the Female Fun label. Female Fun did a whole series of these on CD and vinyl around 2004/2005 from Vol.1 to Vol. 3. This reissue came with a black picture sleeve and featured two additional beats previously unavailable on the original release.

Artist: DJ Spinna
Title: "From Here To There" Instrumentals
Format: 2LP
Producer: DJ Spinna
Label: BBE/Rapster
Year: 2002
Cat#: PR0012 LPI

A real solid release by DJ Spinna featuring an eclectic selection of beats and styles, from House to straight Hip Hop. Album comes in a black sleeve with a white sticker across the top. You don't come across these very often.

Artist: Starving Artists Crew
Title: "Up Pops The Sac" Instrumentals
Format: LP
Producers: Starving Artists Crew
Label: Fat Beats
Year: 2005
Cat#: FB 5110 inst

The Starving Artists Crew has a sound similar to People Under The Stairs and Ugly Duckling. You'll find some of the funkiest production here. Album comes in a picture sleeve.

Artist: Strong Arm Steady
Title: "In Search Of Stoney Jackson" Instrumentals
Format: 2LP
Producer: Madlib
Label: Stones Throw
Year: 2010
Cat#: STH2242

One of the most interesting and solid Hip Hop releases from Stones Throw in recent years. Produced entirely by Madlib. Album comes in a picture sleeve with illustrated cover art.

Artist: Various
Title: "Superappin Vol. II" Instrumentals
Format: 2LP
Producers: Oh No, J Rawls, Kankick, Ge-Ology, Pete Rock, The Are
Label: Grooveattack
Year: 2001
Cat#: GAP082i

In my opinion I think "Superappin II" is much better than the first volume. On the original vocal version for Vol. 2 you'll find guest appearances from artists like Grand Agent, Thrust, J Live, Pete Rock, Maspyke, and The 5 Deez, among many guest MCs. The production for this record was handled by a strong roster of veteran producers. Album comes in a white sleeve with a sticker across the top.

Artist: Swollen Members
Title: "Balance" Instrumentals
Format: 2LP
Producers: Alchemist, Del, Evidence, Joey Chavez, Paul Nice
Label: Battle Axe
Year: 2001
Cat#: BAX 1022-1

"Balance" might be the Swollen Members' best album as far as having a strong selection of beats. How can you go wrong with Joey Chavez, Evidence, Paul Nice, and The Alchemist? Album comes in a red and black picture sleeve.

Artist: Swollen Members
Title: "Bad Dreams" Instrumentals
Format: 2LP
Producers: The Alchemist, Evidence, Rob The Viking, Joey Chavez, Seanski, Nucleus
Label: Battle Axe
Year: 2001
Cat#: BAX1019

Back in 2001, Battle Axe released an instrumental version for the first four Swollen Members albums. The first three albums had the best beats in my opinion, and offered more production from Evidence, Joey Chavez and Paul Nice compared to the fourth LP. The beats on "Bad Dreams," their second album, are pretty solid. Album comes in a picture sleeve.

Artist: Talib Qweli & Hi Tek
Title: "Reflection Eternal" Instrumentals
Format: 2LP
Producer: Hi Tek
Label: Rawkus
Year: 2000
Cat#: RWK1187

It seemed like Rawkus could do no wrong with the type of high quality records they released with artists like Mos Def, Hi Tek, Pharoahe Monch, Black Star, Jurassic 5, Talib Kweli... the list goes on. The many instrumental versions they also released were an added bonus for DJs, like this one for the "Reflection Eternal" LP. Producer Hi Tek was really at the peak of his production creativity and output back during his Rawkus years, and his beats were particularly impressive on this album. Record comes in a generic black sleeve with a sticker in the top left hand corner.

Artist: 3582
Title: "The Living Soul" Instrumentals
Format: 2EP
Producers: J Rawls, Fat Jon
Label: Hum Drums
Year: 2001
Cat#: HD 002

3582 consisted of producers Fat Jon (5 Deez) and J Rawls (Lone Catalysts) behind the microphone as well as behind the beats. The end result is a creative and enthralling journey into dusty sounds and punchy drum programming behind clever word play. The instrumental record is a bonus companion to the vocal disc. Record also comes in a picture sleeve, and you'll find variations of copies with green or orange covers.

Artist: 3582
Title: "Situationalethics" Instrumentals
Format: 2EP
Producers: J Rawls, Fat Jon
Label: Hum Drums
Year: 2001
Cat#: HD 008-1

Same formula as the first 3582 EP, but this time the vocals explored more mature subject matter, like love, passion, and of course, relationships and their problems. Beats were always fat on these EPs. Record comes with a bonus instrumental disc and also a picture sleeve.

Artist: Ugly Duckling
Title: "Bang For The Buck" Instrumentals
Format: 2LP
Producer: Young Einstein
Label: Fat Beats
Year: 2005
Cat#: 659125117-1

I'd love to own an instrumental version to every Ugly Duckling release solely for their funky production style and lush beats. Unfortunately "Bang For The Buck" was the only album we saw with an instrumental version. Album comes in a white picture sleeve.

Artist: Unsung Heroes
Title: "Unleashed" Instrumentals
Format: 2LP
Producers: Unsung Heroes
Label: Scenario
Year: 2000
Cat#: SCINS005

I feel like the Unsung Heroes were largely overlooked and underappreciated for what a solid piece of work their album actually was. The original vocal version released on 75Ark/Scenario had a strong roster of MCs, featuring Siah, & Yeshua Dapo Ed, Rob O, J Live, Godfather Don, Ken Boogaloo, and Frankenstein, just to name a few. They had a similar sound to the Nextmen's production style with bouncy, sample heavy tracks. Instrumental version comes in a plain white sleeve with a sticker in the top right hand corner.

Artist: DJ Vadim
Title: "The Sound Catcher Extras" Instrumentals
Format: 2LP
Producer: DJ Vadim
Label: BBE
Year: 2007
Cat#: BBELP 082

DJ Vadim records are usually filed in the Electronica section in most music shops, but he definitely makes Hip Hop. I don't think most people realize how much Hip Hop gets filed in the Electronica section. Instrumental version for "The Sound Catcher Extras" offers an eclectic range of musical styles and beats. Album comes in a black sleeve with a red sticker across the top.

Artist: Various Blends
Title: "Levitude" Instrumentals
Format: 3LP
Producers: Friz B, Peanut Butter Wolf
Label: Baraka Foundation
Year: 2000
Cat#: BKA 99115 LP

Here's another largely overlooked group from the Bay Area. Their album "Levitude" was a nice departure from the normal sound coming from the Bay, and featured some great production from producer Friz B. You'll also find a couple beats produced by PB Wolf on here. Record comes in a black sleeve with a sticker across the top.

Artist: Various Blends
Title: "Fanna Burn" Instrumentals
Format: 2LP
Producers: Unknown
Label: No Mayo
Year: 2002
Cat#: MNR-106

There have been at least two 12" singles from this album, but I'm uncertain if an actual full-length vocal version of this album is known to exist. A little research turned up that "Fanna Burn" is actually unreleased. Production credits are also unknown, but I imagine Friz B was behind the beats. Album comes in a generic white sleeve and may also be found stashed in a dollar bin somewhere at your local record shop. I know I found a few copies in a dollar bin in the Bay Area.

Artist: Various
Title: "Low Life's Main Courses, Food" Instrumentals
Format: 2LP
Producers: Braintax, Harry Love, C Swing, Jehst, Chester P, Benny Live-O, Iguana Man, Farma G, Otis
Label: Low Life
Year: 2003
Cat#: LOW23LP

I was after this record for a long time. The album, released by Low Life, is an import and features a nice selection of beats from some of Europe's best beatsmiths. Labels are blank like a test pressing, and the album comes in a picture sleeve with a photo of a dinner table loaded with food on the front cover.

Artist: Viktor Vaughn
Title: "Vaudeville Villain" Instrumentals
Format: EP
Producers: RJD2, King Honey, Heat Sensor
Label: Sound Ink
Year: 2011
Cat#: SIK022

This record was the bonus disc from the limited hand-numbered "Gold Edition" re-release for Viktor Vaughn's "Vaudeville Villain" LP. You'll find previously unreleased instrumentals and a cappellas on the orange vinyl disc.

Artist: Wild Child
Title: "Secondary Protocol" Instrumentals
Format: 2LP
Producers: Madlib, Oh No
Label: Stones Throw
Year: 2003
Cat#: STH2070

I wasn't the biggest fan of Wild Child as an MC, but all these instrumental albums from the cronies in the Lootpack are really dope. Album features beats from two of the West Coast's best and most prolific producers. Record comes in a generic black sleeve with yellowish-green labels.

Artist: Will Sessions
Title: "Elmatic" Instrumentals
Format: 2LP
Producer: Sam Beaubien
Label: Fat Beats
Year: 2011
Cat#: FB5149

Elmatic, a clever "Illmatic" inspired tribute album from Elzi (Slum Village) was surprisingly well received by diehard fanatics of Nas's classic 5 mic-rated debut LP. The instrumentals found on this limited edition LP are probably the closest thing you're ever gonna get to an actual instrumental release of "Illmatic," and they stay true to the original sound of those classic beats. Album comes in a picture sleeve.

Artist: Yesh
Title: "Into Fresh Things" Instrumentals
Format: 2EP
Producer: Yesh
Label: Ill Boogie
Year: 2002
Cat#: ILL72049-1

Yesh, from the duo "Siah & Yesua Dapo Ed," released this solid EP for the Ill Boogie Earplug series. A bonus instrumental disc is always included with these Earplug EPs, which is a huge plus for me. Here the instrumentals are driven by the pulse of dusty Jazz samples, crisp drum programming, and the soothing flow of mellow guitar loops. Record comes with a blue picture sleeve.

Artist: Y Society
Title: "Travel At Your Own Pace" Instrumentals
Format: LP
Producer: Damu The Fudgemunk
Label: Redef
Year: 2000
Cat#: RDF004

Limited edition instrumental release of Y Society's critically acclaimed debut album. It carries some brilliant production. Record comes in a plain black sleeve.

Artist: Zion I
Title: "Mind Over Matter" Instrumentals
Format: 2LP
Producer: Zion I
Label: Ground Control
Year: 2000
Cat#: GCR7025

My first encounter with a Zion I record was during my college radio DJ days at KALX in Berkeley. We used to play an impressive promo 12" called "Inner Light" that was unlike anything I had heard before. Their production was equally impressive back then. Zion I really doesn't make songs like this anymore, unfortunately, and those songs from the original 12" release don't appear on the instrumental LP. But there are a lot of other good beats to choose from here. Album comes in a generic black sleeve and can easily be found for around $15 or less — sealed copies, too.

PROMOTIONAL AND SHOW VINYL

All of the records featured in this section were made for promotional use or performance purposes only. Performance discs, or "show vinyl" pressings, are much rarer than your typical promotion-only record. These special pressings (sometimes privately pressed) were never intended to be given to anyone outside of the group or producers, and are almost always pressed in very low numbers. Typically fewer than 100 or even less than 50 copies of some of these exist worldwide.

Artist: Aceyalone
Title: "Book Of Human Language" Instrumentals
Format: 2LP
Producer: Mumbles
Label: Nu Gruv Alliance/GroundControl/Project Blowed
Year: 1998
Cat#: Nu Gruv GCR 7002-12

This particular record is apparently the original instrumental pressing for Aceyalone's "Book Of Human Language" LP, which was pressed years before Mumbles took it upon himself to release these on his own. My best guess is that these were originally show vinyl pressings made for Aceyalone at the time. Record comes in a generic white promo sleeve with a sticker in the top right hand corner.

Artist: Alkaholiks
Title: "Liquidation" Instrumentals
Format: 2LP
Producers: E Swift, Easy Moe Bee, Madlib
Label: Loud
Year: 1997
Cat#: DRAB-67567-1-A

I first saw a bootleg of this record back in '96 or '97, but tracking down an official copy for myself proved to be harder than I ever anticipated. It took many years and a going out of business liquidation by Loud Records to finally land a copy. Here you'll find some early Madlib production. Original copies come in a black promo sleeve with a sticker pasted in the middle of the cover.

Artists: Artifacts
Title: "Between A Rock And A Hard Place" Instrumentals
Format: 2LP
Producers: Buckwild, T-Ray
Label: Big Beat
Year: 1994
Cat#: ST-PR-5793

Here's another rare pressing from the early '90s that still pops up for sale from time to time. There's also at least two bootleg pressings for this one, so beware of those impostors. The official pressings are always specialty test pressings and feature every instrumental from the Artifacts' debut LP. Some of the best golden era production from producers T-Ray and Buckwild are found here. Record comes in a generic white promo sleeve.

Artist: Bahamadia
Title: "Kollage" Instrumentals
Format: LP
Producers: Da Beatminerz, DJ Premier, The Roots, GURU
Label: Chrysalis
Year: 1996
Cat#: SPRO-11616 SRC stamp

I think this record may have been the starting point of my instrumental LP obsession. Surprisingly enough you'll see this record up for auction more often than any other instrumental promo from Crysalis. Because of this, the price has significantly gone down over the years. This record is a must-have for beat fanatics for the level of production from producers like DJ Premier, Da Beatminerz, The Roots and GURU. Promo comes in a generic black sleeve with the gold promo stamp on the cover.

Artist: Bas One
Title: "For The Mentally Astute" Instrumentals
Format: 2LP
Producer: Fanatik
Label: Heratik
Year: 2001
Cat#: S-47418 HTK-021

I don't expect too much from the dollar bins but occasionally I'll come across something interesting in there, like this overlooked gem by Bas One. I discovered this record one night while flipping through the dollar bins at a local shop. It's a white label performance disc produced entirely by Fanatik from Oakland. A prime example of why you should always check the dollar bins! Record comes in a generic white promo sleeve with blank labels. Vocal LP can be found pressed as a triple disc album on colored vinyl.

Artist: The Beatnuts
Title: "Musical Massacre" Instrumentals
Format: LP
Producers: Beatnuts
Label: LOUD
Year: 1999
Cat#: RPRO LP 0934

It took me a while to track down a copy of this record. You see different versions of this LP with different labels, etc., but the white label promo is official. You'll find eight beats on this record. Seven are from the actual album, but one is unfamiliar to me and might be titled "Brothaz on The Streets," judging from the intro during the first minute or so. Record comes in white promo sleeve. I've also seen bootleg versions and reissues for this record.

Artist: Blackalicious
Title: "Blazing Arrow" Instrumentals
Format: 2LP
Producers: Chief Xcel, Cut Chemist, Questlove
Label: MCA
Year: 2002
Cat#: MCAR-257722

Remember the website HipHopSite? They don't sell vinyl anymore, but HipHopSite is where I got my first copy of this record. It came for free with an online purchase I made. Here you'll find production by Cut Chemist (Jurassic 5), Chief Xcel, and Questlove from The Roots. As a promo this record is pretty common, and it's easily obtainable for less than ten bucks. Comes in black promo sleeve with a sticker pasted in the middle of the cover.

Artist: Bumpy Knuckles
Title: "Industry Shakedown" Instrumentals
Format: 2LP
Producers: Pete Rock, DJ Premier, Diamond D, Alchemist, Freddie Foxxx
Label: KJAC
Year: 2000
Cat#: KJAC-INST-1

When this record first appeared on eBay a few years ago people went nuts; in the end it sold for over $200. Since then more and more copies have gone up for sale and the price has significantly dropped. It's definitely a good record to have in your collection if you ever come across it. It's show vinyl, unreleased, and features beats from a roster of highly respected producers: DJ Premier, Pete Rock, The Alchemist and Diamond D all worked on this record. Record has blank white labels and comes in white promo sleeves.

Artist: Da Bush Babees
Title: "Ambushed" Instrumentals
Format: LP
Producers: JP, Salaam Remi, Ali Shaheed Muhamed, Jermaine Duprie, Nikke Nikole
Label: Reprise
Year: 1994
Cat# PRO A 7214 A SRC stamp

Da Bush Babees released a couple of really solid albums in the early '90s. This particular instrumental LP from them is quite rare, and features eight beats from their debut album, "Ambushed." In all the years I've been buying records I've only seen one other copy of this one, sold at auction a few years ago. That one had the regular blue/yellow promo label you'll see on other Bush Babees releases. This is the first white label version I've ever come across. Record comes in a generic white promo sleeve. No known bootlegs exist for this record.

Artist: Das Efx
Title: "Hold It Down" Instrumentals
Format: 2LP
Producers: DJ Premier, Pete Rock., Easy Moe Bee, Clark Kent
Label: East West
Year: 1995
Cat#: ED 5810

You wouldn't think that this record was instrumental just by glancing at the label, but that's how some of these instrumental records are. They can be very ambiguous, so it helps to know what to look for, like matrix numbers and label design. Here you'll find beats from Pete Rock, DJ Premier, Easy Moe Bee and Clark Kent. Record comes in generic white promo sleeve.

Artist: Dead Prez
Title: "Let's Get Free" Instrumentals
Format: 2LP
Producers: Hedrush. Lord Jamar
Label: Loud
Year: 2000
Cat#: RPROLP4376

This particular record is another one that doesn't pop up too often, or that normally fetches a lot of money. But the album definitely offers a solid selection of beats. You may be familiar with one of the beats featured on this record — the instrumental for a song called "Hip Hop" was regularly played on the Dave Chapelle Show aired by Comedy Central. Album comes in black promo sleeve with the Loud Records logo on the front and back cover.

Artist: Del The Funky Homosapien
Title: "No Need For Alarm" Instrumentals
Format: 2LP
Producers: Domino, Snupe, Jay Biz, A-Plus. Casual, SD50's
Label: Elektra
Year: 1993
Cat#: STED 5680 A1

This record remained an unconfirmed rumor for many years until I accidentally found a copy at a local shop in 2007. Best four dollars I've ever spent! Show vinyl contains all the beats (except "Wack M.C.'s") from Del's sophomore LP. I found out later from a member of the group that Elektra made a mistake and left that instrumental off the record. The track listing for this one is also out of its normal order. It's rumored to have a pressing number of less than 100 copies.

Artist: Del The Funky Homosapien
Title: "No Need For Alarm" Instrumentals
Format: 2LP
Producers: Domino, Snupe, Jay Biz, A-Plus, Casual, SD50's
Label: Elektra
Year: 1993
Cat#: ED 5680

Here's what a finished promo for the instrumental record looks like. This particular copy was found at a small record show here in Oakland a couple years ago, unfortunately with the second disc (sides c/d) missing. It's the only other copy I've ever seen with the completed promo label. Very rare.

Artist: Diamond
Title: "Hatred, Passions, And Infidelity" Instrumentals
Format: 2LP
Producers: Diamond D, Buckwild, Kid Capri
Label: Mercury
Year: 1997
Cat#: MELP 172

For a Diamond D promo, you'd think this album would be a hard one to track down, but it's not. It's extremely common to find a copy in stores or online for $10 or less. I swear I see this record almost every time I go record shopping. Maybe most people think it's just a regular promo of the vocal album because they look identical. If you come across one, make sure the record says "Instrumental Vinyl" in micro print underneath the Diamond logo on the cover sticker. Record comes in black promo sleeve with a bright red sticker in the top right hand corner.

Artist: Digable Planets
Title: "Reachin (A New Refutation Of Time And Space)" Instrumentals
Format: 2LP
Producer: Butterfly
Year: 1993
Label: Pendulum Elektra
Cat#: ED 5647 SRC

This rare piece is the instrumental performance disk (or tour vinyl) for the Digable Planets debut album. It's interesting to compare the original album to this one. You'll notice that some of the layers on the beats here are peeled away. For example, a bass line might be turned down or missing, or a drum, maybe a hi-hat or two, was removed or turned down on a track. This was done to allow a live band to fill in the gaps on stage. Record comes in a generic white gatefold sleeve.

Artist: Easy Moe Bee
Title: "Now Or Never: Odyssey 2000" Instrumentals
Format: 2LP
Producer: Easy Moe Bee
Label: Priority
Year: 2000
Cat#: 04992-81395-1-A

As an overall album "Odyssey 2000" was kind of hit or miss vocally, even though the album featured a lot of worthy artist appearances such as Gang Starr. Production wise, though, Easy Moe Bee is a legend on the boards and brings a lot to the table with his beats, making this instrumental version an essential one to have in the collection. Record comes in a generic white promo sleeve.

Artist: Edo G
Title: "Life Of A Kid In The Ghetto" Instrumentals
Format: LP
Producers: Joe Mansfield, Teddy Ted, Special K
Label: PWL America
Year: 1991
Cat#: PWL 88931 A

This one right here is definitely one of my favorite instrumental records in the collection. It's very unusual to see any album from the '90s in instrumental form, and "Life Of A Kid In The Ghetto" is a certified classic and a favorite of mine since high school. I was told these records were used strictly for live shows and a very small number of them were ever pressed. Record comes in a generic black promo sleeve with a PWL stamp on the label.

Artist: Ed OG
Title: "Roxbury 02119" Instrumentals
Format: 2LP
Producers: Diamond D, Joe Mansfield
Label: Chemistry
Year: 1993
Cat#: CR-PROMO-INST-1

Originally the Roxbury album was a promo-only pressing that came in a black sleeve with a small sticker pasted on the front. It's arguably his best work, and is still a very sought after piece of vinyl that consistently sells for $70-$100 and up. The instrumental version is even harder to find, but it's not as desired as the original vocal LP. These were pressed strictly for live performances. You'll find all the beats from the Roxbury LP on two discs. Album comes in a generic black promo sleeve with blank labels.

Artist: Funkdoobiest
Title: "Brothas Doobie" Instrumentals
Format: LP
Producers: DJ Muggs, Ralph M, DJ Lethal, Buckwild
Label: Immortal
Year: 1995
Cat#: S-31812

If I'm not mistaken, this may be the only instrumental pressing Immortal Records ever issued. Immortal was a solid label back in the mid to late '90s and released a load of Funkdoobiest promos and various other records, usually on colored vinyl. This particular record is one-of-a-kind, though, and doesn't come around very often. Here you'll find every instrumental from Funkdoobiest's sophomore release, "Brothas Doobie," including the coveted Buckwild remix instrumental for "Dedicated" that was absent on the original 12" release and can only be found here on this promo LP.

Artist: Genius/GZA
Title: "Liquid Swords" Instrumentals
Format: 2LP
Producer: RZA
Label: Geffen
Year: 1995
Cat#: PRO-A2-4810

It took me at least ten years to find a copy of this record after discovering one in a DJ's crate back in '95. Geffen only pressed a couple of these instrumental albums for their artists back then, with "Liquid Swords" being the most sought after LP for obvious reasons— it's a major classic. This record has been bootlegged before, so beware of fakes. The original promo labels will have a small circle around the spindle hole, which was a typical characteristic of Geffen pressings at that time.

Artist: Ghostface Killah
Title: "Iron Man" Instrumentals
Format: 2LP
Producer: RZA
Label: Razor Sharp
Year: 1996
Cat#: RS003

Here's a record that I was never really sure actually existed until one popped up at auction a few years ago and ended up selling for over $300. I've seen a few sealed copies selling for less than $60 since then, though, and they seem to show up more often now. Record has also been bootlegged to death so watch out for fakes. Record comes in a plain white promo sleeve and released on Razor Sharp records. The instrumental for the CD-only cut "Marvel" is also on here.

Artist: Ghostface Killah
Title: "Supreme Clientele" Instrumentals
Format: 2LP
Producers: RZA, Juju, Inspectah Deck, Ghostface
Label: Epic
Year: 2000
Cat#: E2S 12700

The most common instrumental promo from Ghostface Killah for some odd reason. It's an unreleased record of an album considered to be one of, if not the best Ghostface album he ever recorded, but I always see this one up for sale on eBay for less than $20. Record comes in a white promo sleeve with a blue and silver sticker in the top right hand corner. Beware of bootleg copies with generic labels.

Artist: Goodie Mob
Title: "Soul Food" Instrumentals
Format: 2LP
Producers: Organized Noise
Label: Laface
Year: 1995
Cat#: LFLP-6024

Goodie Mob's "Soul Food" has some nice production the album. This particular pressing on the Laface label is also pretty common for a promo. Since it's a pressing by a major label, I'd imagine they pressed at least a few thousand of these. Album comes in black Laface promo sleeve.

Artist: Goodie Mob
Title: "World Party" Instrumentals
Format: 2LP
Producers: Organized Noise, Easy Moe Bee
Label: Laface
Year: 2000
Cat#: LFLP-6064

Goodie Mob's third installment is a little more out there and polished compared to their previous releases, but I found a couple really nice beats on here. I probably wouldn't have checked for this one either if I didn't receive a copy in my stash of records from the record pool one day. Record comes in black Laface promo sleeve.

Artist: Grand Puba
Title: "Reel To Reel" Instrumentals
Format: 2LP
Producers: Grand Puba, SD50's
Label: Elektra
Year: 1992
Cat#: ED 5633

Grand Puba broke off from Brand Nubian in the early '90s and released his first solo LP with Elektra in 1992. In those early years Elektra pressed only a few promotional instrumental records, which were next to impossible to find without connections back then. I'm still after a copy of "Mecca & The Soul Brother"! Of course, this one has been bootlegged a few times as well. Always look for the SRC stamp in the dead wax on the original pressings. Album comes in a generic white gatefold sleeve.

Artist: GURU
Title: "Jazzmatazz Vol. 1" Instrumentals
Format: LP
Producer: GURU
Label: Crysalis
Year: 1993
Cat#: SPRO 10428 A. SRC

Obtaining records off of a retired DJ (especially a DJ known for having music industry connections) is a good way to find rare pressings, like this one by GURU. In all my years of buying records I've never come across this one. Even every photo I've found online has been of an import version or a bootleg, so it's very rare. Here you'll find ten beats from the classic album by GURU. Record comes in a generic white promo sleeve.

Artist: GURU
Title: "Jazzmatazz Vol. II" Instrumentals
Format: 2LP
Producers: DJ Premier, GURU, Solsonics
Label: Chrysalis
Year: 1995
Cat#: SPRO-10429-A

Specialty's test pressings have become known like no other recognizable label for rare golden era hits and unreleased treats, like this "Jazzmatazz" LP on Crysalis. Here you'll find all the beautifully crafted instrumentals for GURU's sophomore journey into Jazz-infused Hip Hop. Record comes in a generic white promo sleeve. Beware of bootleg versions; always look for the SRC stamp in the dead wax.

Artist: Harvey Lindo
Title: "Kid Gloves" Instrumentals
Format: LP
Producers: Harvey Lindo
Label: Planetgroove
Year: 2005
Cat#: LOUD

I'm forever grateful to my man Sadie for hooking me up with this rare Japanese promo on the Planetgroove Label. All the beats from Lindo's solid "Kid Gloves" LP are here. Record comes in a white promo sleeve with blank labels. One label is stamped with the Planetgroove logo.

Artist: Ice T
Title: "Rhyme Pays" Instrumentals
Format: LP
Producers: Afrika Islam, David Storrs
Year: 1987
Label: Sire White Label
Cat:# 1 -25602 -A -BGT - SH3 B-28946-SH3 18052 1-1 Sterling

Sometimes amazing stories come with the records you buy, like the story behind this record as told by the seller I bought it from. He said he found this album in a fore-closed storage locker he purchased that was apparently once owned by Ice T. I'd never seen this one before I found the seller; it's the lost instrumental performance disc for Ice T's debut album on Sire, called "Rhyme Pays." A legendary record score right there. Record comes in a generic white promo sleeve.

Artist: Inspectah Deck
Title: "Uncontrolled Substance" Instrumentals
Format: 2LP
Producers: 4th Disciple, Pete Rock, RZA, True Master
Label: Loud
Year: 1999
Cat#: LOUD REC INSP DECK A

I think most people believe this record is a bootleg because of the way the label looks. It doesn't look like the typical release on Loud Records, but I'm almost 100% positive that this record isn't a boot. The vinyl looks consistent with other Loud promos I've come across and the overall vinyl and sound quality indicate that it's legitimate. You also have the mastering mark of "dcharles" in the runout. There's also a rare Mobb Deep instrumental LP with the same type of label and catalog description that this one has. Record comes in a generic white promo sleeve.

Artist: Kardinal Offishall
Title: "Quest For Fire: Firestarter Vol.1" Instrumentals
Format: 2LP
Producers: Kardinal Offishall, Saukrates, Mr. Attic
Label: MCA
Year: 2001
Cat#: UMCR-4360-1

Kardinall Offishall was part of the spike in quality records coming out of Toronto, Canada during the mid to late '90s. Beside him, artists like Thrust, Frankenstein, The Grassroots and Saukrates all released quality records on small private labels. This instrumental record was pressed by MCA/Figure IV Canada as a promo-only release for the "Quest For Fire" LP. Overall it's not the most enjoyable record, but all is not lost here. You'll still find a few really nice beats. Record comes in a generic black promo sleeve.

Artist: Killah Priest
Title: "Heavy Mental" Instrumentals
Format: 2LP
Producers: 4th Disciple, Killah Priest, True Master
Label: Geffen
Year: 1998
Cat#: PRO-A2-1162-RE1

This particular record is very underappreciated in my opinion. As a Wu Tang affili-ated promo-only record, you'd think it would be much harder to find, but I've come across this one many times priced for less than ten bucks. If you come across a copy remember this bit of info: I've heard this from a few people that apparently some of these records have the instrumental label, but are actually mislabeled clean vocal versions. I'm happy to say I haven't had that problem yet. Record comes in a plain white promo sleeve.

Elektra

OL' DIRTY BASTARD
RETURN TO THE 36 CHAMBERS:
THE DIRTY VERSION INSTRUMENTAL

STEREO
33 1/3 RPM

1. SHIMMY SHIMMY YA (2-46)
2. BABY C'MON (3-39)
3. BROOKLYN ZOO (3-50)
4. HIPPA TO DA HOPPA (2-47)

ED 5739
SIDE A

Artist: Lewis Parker
Title: "Masquerades & Sillhouettes" Instrumentals
Format: LP
Producer: Lewis Parker
Label: Melankolik
Year: 1998
Cat#: JEDI1A

I was really fortunate to acquire a copy of this rare record directly from Lewis Parker a few years ago off of eBay. It's the original instrumental show vinyl for his "Masquerades & Silhouettes" LP. The record has a fraction of the beats you'll find on the World Of Dusty Vinyl reissue, but it doesn't really matter too much. It's still an incredible record. LP has blank labels and was also signed by Lewis Parker on the inner sleeve.

Artist: Little Brother
Title: "The Minstrel Show" Instrumentals
Format: 2LP
Producer: 9th Wonder
Label: Atlantic
Year: 2005
Cat#: PR 302001

This was another largely underappreciated album by Little Brother. 9th Wonder's soulful production also makes this one another favorite of mine. Shortly after the release of this album the group disbanded and all pursued successful solo careers. Record comes in the Atlantic promo sleeve with a red arrow pointing down.

Artist: DJ Mitsu The Beats
Title: "New Awakening" Instrumentals
Format: 2LP
Producer: DJ Mitsu The Beats
Label: Planet Groove
Year: 2003
Cat#: PGLP-P1001

Apparently this record was exclusively sold at the Jazzy Sport record shop in Japan, where of course it was sold out when I first stumbled across it. I don't even remember how I obtained my copy. But here it is— the full instrumental version of DJ Mitsu's debut album on Planetgroove. Record comes in a thick card stock cover reminiscent of those old records from the 1960s and '70s. Inside is a line sheet with track listing and other album info. The labels are blank and stamped on one side with "Jazzy Sport Music Shop." Production is top notch.

Artist: Mobb Deep
Title: "Hell On Earth" Instrumentals
Format: 2LP
Producers: Mobb Deep
Label: Loud
Year: 1996
Cat#: RDAB-67432-1-A

Here's one of the more extraordinary instrumental promos pressed by Loud Records. You really don't see this one very often, if at all, so if you see a copy you have to pick it up. The record comes in a black promo sleeve with a bright yellow sticker on the top right hand corner. The label says "TV Tracks," which isn't really the correct description for this record. TV track usually means vocals float in and out of the music like a hype man on stage. There's some of that, but for the most part these are all instrumental tracks.

Artist: DJ Muro
Title: "Pan Rhythm Flight No. 11154" Instrumentals
Format: 2LP
Producers: Muro, Pete Rock, Diamond D
Label: Incredible
Year: 2000
Cat#: PRT-371

Overall a solid record by Japan's most famous beat artist. I think most people seek this record out for the exclusive Diamond D produced track, "Lyrical Tyrants," and the Incredible "Patch Up The Pieces," produced by Pete Rock. Those two cuts alone make this a highly sought after promotional gem from Japan. Record comes in a blue Incredible Records promo sleeve.

Artist: Nas
Title: "Stillmatic" Instrumentals
Format: 2LP
Producers: Large Professor, DJ Premier, Salaam Remi
Label: Columbia
Year: 2002
Cat#: C2S 56856

I keep wishing the label said "Illmatic Instrumentals" instead of "Stillmatic." That would've been incredible, but I'll take this one. There's still a nice selection of beats on here from DJ Premier, Large Professor and Salaam Remi. Record comes in bright red promo sleeve. Original pressing also has a bright red label to match. Beware of bootlegs — there's at least one bootleg of this record out there with a cheap looking off-white label.

Artist: Nas
Title: "God's Son" Instrumentals
Format: 2LP
Producers: Salaam Remi, Alchemist
Label: Columbia
Year: 2003
Cat#: C2S 59073

This particular instrumental promo is the more common record of the two released under Columbia by Nas. I've seen it many times before while out digging for records. There's also a promo a cappella version for this LP, which is more scarce than the instrumental version. Both come in the trademark bright red Columbia promo sleeves. You'll find some decent beats on here.

Artist: Ol' Dirty Bastard
Title: "Return To The 36 Chambers" Instrumentals
Format: 2LP
Producer: RZA
Label: Elektra
Year: 1995
Cat#: ED-5739

I found a guy selling a copy of this who told me he worked at Elektra during the year these were pressed up and that he'd had a copy sitting on his shelf, unplayed, ever since. He wasn't lying when he said it was unplayed; when I got it, the record looked like it hadn't been touched since the day it left Elektra's doorstep. If you find a copy be aware that these instrumentals have also been bootlegged. The bootleg has the same label, but it's off-white compared to the original and it looks sloppy. The original will also always have the SRC stamp in the run out groove.

Artist: Outkast
Title: "ATLiens" Instrumentals
Format: 2LP
Producers: Organized Noise, Outkast
Label: Laface
Year: 1996
Cat#: LFLP-6033

Outkast was a highly successful group who managed to create hits with every record they released. I remember "Elevators" getting heavy rotation on our college radio station back when I was there. Usually college radio stayed away from songs that were played on commercial radio, but this one seemed to fit right in with the college radio format. This promo is fairly common and you can easily find it priced very cheap. Record comes in black Laface promo sleeve.

Artist: Outkast
Title: "Aquemini" Instrumentals
Format: 3LP
Producers: Organized Noise, Outkast
Label: Laface
Year: 1998
Cat#: LFL-6056

Here's another record I kept seeing bootlegs for, but never an actual promo copy. I'm almost positive that I received a copy of this from the record pool, too, but assumed it was a clean version and dumped it. Definitely a mistake if I did. I think most people like myself just didn't know what they had with this one. Promo comes in the typical black Laface promo sleeve. If you find one, check the catalog number. In fact, memorize the catalog number. This is a good record to have.

Artist: Pete Rock & CL Smooth
Title: "The Main Ingredient" Instrumentals
Format: 2LP
Producer: Pete Rock
Label: Elektra
Year: 1994
Cat#: ED 5708

I remember both of the Pete Rock instrumental LPs being sort of mythical records. We never saw anything real outside of the usual bootlegs. Not a photo of an actual copy, nobody I knew had one, nothing! That's how rare these were. I still haven't found a copy of "Mecca," but I'll take "The Main Ingredient." It's definitely one of my favorite records of all time. There are many bootleg copies of this record, so look out for those. The original comes in a generic white promo sleeve with the tan Elektra labels. The SRC stamp also appears in the runout groove.

Artist: The Pharcyde
Title: "Bizarre Ride II The Pharcyde" Instrumentals
Format: LP
Producers: J Swift, LA Jay, Tre Hardson
Label: Test Pressing
Year: 1993
Cat#: S-27242 005A

I picked this up from a dealer who told me he bought it in a record shop in Southern California back in '96. At the time I didn't know there was actual show vinyl for the Pharcyde's first album — I assumed, but I had never actually seen a copy before. I purchased the record and discovered that the instrumentals are slightly different from the Delicious Vinyl pressing. The instrumental to "Pack The Pipe" is also on here, which was unavailable on any other promotional record or commercial release that I knew of. Record comes in a generic white promo sleeve.

Artist: Public Enemy
Title: "Muse Sick-N-Hour Mess Age" Instrumentals
Format: 2LP
Producers: The Bomb Squad
Label: Def Jam
Year: 1994
Cat#: 314-523-399-1DJ

I purchased this record from a guy for only ten bucks. These typically sell for around $40 or more, so I asked him why was he selling it for so cheap and he told me the first song skipped on all four records. When the record arrived, it looked unplayed. No skips either! Gotta love that. This promo is a good one to have. You get four records: the first half is vocal and the second half is instrumental. You won't find the instrumentals on the commercial release. Album comes in a gatefold picture sleeve. Artwork is in greyscale.

Artist: Q-Tip
Title: "Amplified" Instrumentals
Format: 2LP
Producers: Jaydee, Q-Tip, DJ Scratch
Label: Arista
Year: 1999
Cat#: ARLP-4619

I don't think I fully appreciated the "Amplified" album when it first came out. I guess like most people I just wasn't ready for a solo album by Q-Tip of the legendary Native Tongues without Phife and Mr. Muhamed. But the album is solid and the production is top notch. You really can't go wrong with Ummah beats. Record comes in a blue Arista promo sleeve.

Artist: Raekwon
Title: "Only Built 4 Cuban Linx" Instrumentals
Format: 2LP
Producer: RZA
Label: Wu Tang
Year: 1995
Cat#: WUTANG011 STERLING

I'm pretty certain this is the rarest Raekwon record of all time. I've never seen another copy of this one before. When I asked Raekwon about this record via Twitter, he said he thought they'd all been destroyed. It was pressed on Wu Tang Records, mostly likely as a performance disc with all the instrumentals for Raekwon's debut album. The label on disc one is identical to the label on disc two. It also has the STERLING mastering stamp in the runout groove. Record has been bootlegged many times already.

Artist: Raekwon
Title: "Immobilarity" Instrumentals
Format: 2LP
Producers: Pete Rock, Jugrnaut, Mike D, Tryflin
Label: Loud
Year: 1999
Cat#: RPROLP 4346

"Immobilarity" wasn't really one of my favorite albums by the Chef Raekwon, but there are still some hits on there. One particular standout that comes to mind is "Sneakers," produced by none other than the Soul Brother #1 Pete Rock. That one is really dope. Record comes in a black Loud Records promo sleeve.

Artist: Sadat X
Title: "Wild Cowboys" Instrumentals
Format: 2LP
Producers: Buckwild, Da Beatminerz, Diamond D, Pete Rock, Showbiz
Label: Loud
Year: 1996
Cat#: RDAB-66970-1-A

I was really surprised when I first learned about an official promo pressing for this record, complete with picture sleeve. It's very unusual for any promo record like this one to use the same cover art work as the vocal LP. The only differences are the missing barcode on the back cover and the word "instrumentals" printed in the bottom left hand corner. Beware of bootleg copies out there in plain black sleeves with blank labels.

Artist: 7L & Esoteric
Title: "Soul Purpose" Instrumentals
Format: 2LP
Producers: The Are, DJ Spinna, Joc Max, 7L, Vinyl Reanimators
Label: Direct
Year: 2001
Cat#: DR-INSTR-1

This particular record is the show vinyl for 7L & Esoteric's brilliant "Soul Purpose" LP. This is a rare piece featuring instrumentals by DJ Spinna, 7L, The Vinyl Reanimators, The Are and Joc Max. When I compared this record to the original vocal LP, I found a couple of beats that might be bonus beats or beats from skits found on the CD version. I'm not really sure, but they sure don't appear on the original vocal LP. Record comes in a white promo sleeve with blank labels. I was told that only 30 copies of this records were made.

Artist: Souls Of Mischief
Title: "No Man's Land" Instrumentals
Format: 2LP
Producers: A Plus, Tajai, Opio, Del, Jay Biz, Snupe,Touré
Label: Jive
Year: 1996
Cat# SOM-2-A SRC

Hiero is known for pressing instrumental records like these for performance purposes only. I'm still after at least two of them. After I found this one I did some research. Domino mentioned that when these were made, he charmed the production woman at Jive to press these up even though Souls Of Mischief had just been dropped from the label. That's why these don't have the Jive logo on them. Only about 75 copies of this record were ever made. Record comes in a white promo sleeve.

Artist: Walkin' Large
Title: "Self" Instrumentals
Format: LP
Producer: Roe Beardie
Label: Warner Germany
Year: 1999
Cat#: PRO6461 B921647-01 A1 KL

Walkin' Large were one of those random imported groups from Europe with really nice beats and an impressive roster of guest features on their albums and 12" singles. Some of their records had production by Lord Finesse and The Roots. Their records are definitely worth seeking out if you're into that '90s sound. Record comes in a generic white promo sleeve.

Artist: Wu Tang Clan
Title: "Wu Tang Forever" Instrumentals
Format: 2LP
Producers: RZA, 4th Disciple, Inspectah Deck, True Master
Label: White
Year: 1997
Cat#: WU-2A-1A RJ

I recently found this in the used bin of a record store down in San Jose, California, priced for only four bucks. I figured that I had something here when I found it; typically show vinyl will have simple labels with minimal or no information printed on them like this, which raised a flag. My gamble ultimately payed off, as it was indeed an instrumental LP. I've seen bootlegs of these instrumentals before but never a record like this one. The overall sound and vinyl quality look and feels right. Record comes in a generic white promo sleeve.

Artist: Xzibit
Title: "40 Dayz & 40 Nightz" Instrumentals
Format: 2LP
Producers: E Swift, Sir Jinx, A Kid Called Roots
Label: Loud
Year: 1998
Cat#: RDAB-67702-1

The first copy I ever found of this was broken: one disc had a huge piece missing from the edge of the record, as if someone had dropped it on the floor. Unfortunately, I didn't find another copy of this one for at least ten years. Now I always see this record. They're like roaches. It's a good record, though, and worth picking up if you come across one. Album comes in black sleeve with a Loud promo sticker pasted in the middle of the cover. This album has also been bootlegged several times.

TOUR PRESSING

ED 5647

ECORD 1
SIDE B

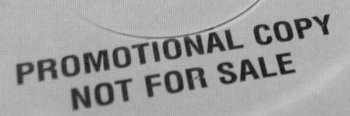

PROMOTIONAL COPY
NOT FOR SALE

five deez kommunicator

THE FOREIGN EXCHANGE CONNECTED INSTRUMENTALS

YELLOW TAPE INSTRUMENTALS

THE INSTRUMENTALS

Grooveman Spot a.k.a. DJ KOU-G ETERNAL DEVELOPMENT INSTRUMENTALS

TOMMY BOY /// DE LA SOUL /// ART OFFICIAL INTELLIGENCE: MOSAIC THUMP /// INSTRUMENTAL VERSION /// TB 1437

the SAMPLER volume 1

FIVE DEEZ KOOLMOTOR

instrumentals

MADVILLAIN

"...ODEST FIVE STARS IN THE GALAXY"

GET

systems

JDILLA RUFF DRAFT BEATS

EASY MO BEE

NOW OR NEVER: ODYSSEY 2000
THE INSTRUMENTALS
STRICTLY FOR THE REAL HEADS

NOW OR NEVER:
ODYSSEY 2000
The Album
In Stores Now

SIDE A

Now or Never	Easy Mo Bee	4:34
Sunstroke	Sauce Money feat. Da Ranjahs & G da K	3:46
Fie Fie Delish	Goodie Mobb	:38
Instrumental No. 1	Easy Mo Bee	4:46
S---'s Goin' Down Tonite	Da Nation feat. Kurupt	

SPRO 81395 ℗ © 2000 Priority Records
Manufactured by Priority Records.
P.O. Box 2590, Los Angeles, CA
Unauthorized duplication is a violation
of applicable laws. All rights reserved.
For promotional use only. Not for sale.

PRIORITY
records

CREDITS

I'd like to send a special "thank you" to my closest friends and family for believing in me and encouraging all of my creative ideas, no matter how crazy those ideas seemed. Also to my son; you're the best thing that has ever happened to me, and some day these records will be yours.

Mr. Krum for the cover design.

Richard Smith at Slice of Spice for being a solid dude.

Jose Morales for the CD design.

DJ Spair for the mix.

And Gingko Press for the chance of a lifetime. Thank you!